The Teacher Quality Index

A Protocol for Teacher Selection

James H. Stronge
Jennifer L. Hindman

Association for Supervision and Curriculum Development
Alexandria, Virginia USA

Association for Supervision and Curriculum Development
1703 N. Beauregard St. • Alexandria, VA 22311–1714 USA
Phone: 800-933-2723 or 703-578-9600 • Fax: 703-575-5400
Web site: www.ascd.org • E-mail: member@ascd.org
Author guidelines: www.ascd.org/write

Gene R. Carter, *Executive Director;* Nancy Modrak, *Director of Publishing;* Julie Houtz, *Director of Book Editing & Production;* Katie Martin, *Project Manager;* Shelley Kirby, *Graphic Designer;* Cynthia Stock, *Typesetter;* Dina Murray Seamon, *Production Specialist/Team Lead*

All Web links in this book are correct as of the publication date below but may have become inactive or otherwise modified since that time. If you notice a deactivated or changed link, please e-mail books@ascd.org with the words "Link Update" in the subject line. In your message, please specify the Web link, the book title, and the page number on which the link appears.

PAPERBACK ISBN-13: 978-1-4166-0272-9   ASCD product # 105001   s2/06
PAPERBACK ISBN-10: 1-4166-0272-0
Also available as an e-book through ebrary, netLibrary, and many online booksellers (see Books in Print for the ISBNs).

Quantity discounts for the paperback edition only: 10–49 copies, 10%; 50+ copies, 15%; for 1,000 or more copies, call 800-933-2723, ext. 5634, or 703-575-5634. For desk copies: MEMBER@ascd.org.

Library of Congress Cataloging-in-Publication Data

Stronge, James H.
    The teacher quality index : a protocol for teacher selection / James H. Stronge, Jennifer L. Hindman.
        p.   cm.
    Includes bibliographical references and index.
    ISBN-13: 978-1-4166-0272-9 (alk. paper)
    ISBN-10: 1-4166-0272-0 (alk. paper)
    1. Teachers—Selection and appointment. 2. Teachers—Rating of. I. Hindman, Jennifer L., 1971–
II. Title.
    LB2835.S77 2006
    379.1'57—dc22

                                                                                2005029633

12 11 10 09 08 07 06   12 11 10 9 8 7 6 5 4 3 2 1

To Kaz
James H. Stronge

To my parents, Andy and Elaine Lilliston,
who taught me the value of asking questions and listening
carefully to the answers.
Jennifer L. Hindman

and

To human resources personnel, instructional leaders, teachers,
and parents who participate in the interview process to identify
and secure effective teachers for every student.

The Teacher Quality Index

A Protocol for Teacher Selection

Acknowledgments

This book is the product of our desire to contribute to improved teacher-selection decisions. Specifically, our intent is to offer a research-based and value-added interview process in which each question solicits information about an applicant's potential for on-the-job success. Initial interest in the topic expressed by various professional associations, school districts, and individuals encouraged us in our work.

We appreciate the support from individuals at ASCD, especially Scott Willis, who recognized the value in the earlier work, *Qualities of Effective Teachers*. Additionally, we would like to acknowledge Megan Tschannen-Moran of the College of William and Mary, who asked insightful questions about the interview protocol during the early development of our study and offered suggestions for making the tables more reader friendly. We also would like to thank Leslie Grant, whose careful review and editing helped to refine the book. Finally, thank you to all the readers who are willing to explore a new tool applied to an old challenge: selecting the best teachers for our classrooms.

Introduction

One of the most critical elements in the success of any school is the quality of teaching that occurs every day in every classroom. If we want students to succeed to their maximum potential, having a quality teacher working with every student is paramount. For this reason, recruiting, selecting, inducting, and sustaining highly effective teachers is one of the greatest challenges facing today's educational leaders.

Research repeatedly has shown that students who are taught by effective teachers achieve more academically than their peers who are taught by less effective teachers (Mendro, Jordon, Gomez, Anderson, & Bembry, 1998; Sanders & Horn, 1998; Stronge & Ward, 2002). In the United States, identifying highly qualified teachers as defined by the No Child Left Behind (NCLB) Act is certainly a major step in the direction of better schooling. However, if we want to maximize the impact of the hiring process, we need to actively look for, identify, and hire teacher applicants who exhibit what research indicates to be the qualities of effective teachers.

The purpose of this book is to provide tools for human resource specialists, school administrators, and others involved in teacher selection to use in accomplishing the important task of hiring effective teachers. The key feature that we provide is the Teacher Quality Index (TQI), a two-part, research-based and field-tested interview protocol for teacher selection.

Before turning to tools for use in the teacher selection process (and the TQI in particular), let's begin with a review of two key background issues: *why we need effective teachers* and *why we have a shortage of effective teachers*.

Why We Need Effective Teachers

Policy, practice, and research all suggest that teachers have a significant impact on the education of their students. No Child Left Behind (Public Law 107-110) mandates that all students in every school in the United States be taught by highly qualified teachers by 2005–2006. Highly qualified teachers are defined as professionals who have been licensed to teach in their respective state (U. S. Department of Education, 2002). Individual states have interpreted this legislation further. For example, the Virginia Department of Education (2002) has defined highly qualified teachers as those who are both certified and teaching in their area or areas of endorsement.

Being certified to teach, however, does not guarantee that a teacher will be successful with students. Students need effective teachers, but the criteria for teacher effectiveness are not as easily defined—or identified—as those for "highly qualified" teachers. In describing teacher effectiveness, a teacher's certification is only one of many components. Teacher effectiveness is a multifaceted concept incorporating all aspects of teachers' backgrounds, skills, and dispositions, ranging from personality to knowledge to technical skills.

The difficulty in identifying effective teachers during the hiring process is compounded by the fact that interviews are seldom conducted in a manner that researchers would deem valid or reliable. The selection process is influenced by the hiring administrators' personal perceptions of what constitutes a good teacher. For some, a good teacher is one who does not refer students to the office for discipline problems; for others, a good teacher is one whose students achieve a grade level or more in academic growth each year. We would be better served if definitions of and decisions regarding teacher effectiveness were informed and guided by available research.

Research-guided decisions yield many benefits, including higher student achievement results, fewer discipline issues, and better relationships between teachers and students (Ralph, Kesten, Lang, & Smith, 1998). Moreover, researchers have found that the teacher impact on student learning lasts for years after students have left the teacher's classroom (Sanders & Horn, 1998). Thus, given these short-term and long-term benefits, school administrators need a well-developed knowledge-base and research-based skills to distinguish effective teacher applicants from others in the candidate pool.

The goal for everyone involved in the hiring process should be placing a highly qualified and highly effective teacher in front of every student in the school. It is true that many teachers grow in their effectiveness over time, but "the best opportunity a principal has to improve teaching and learning in a school is when a new teacher is hired" (Donaldson, 1990, p. 1). This is because a decision can be made about an applicant's effectiveness without spending a single staff development dollar on the teacher. Thus, school leaders can use the selection process to evaluate applicants in order to determine which ones are likely to make a profoundly positive difference in the lives of students.

Why We Have a Shortage of Effective Teachers

Employees do not magically appear when the need arises; they must be recruited, selected, and retained. The recruitment of individuals into the teaching profession is the first step in securing an effective teacher for every classroom (Dozier & Bertotti, 2000). Selecting the most qualified applicants is the second challenge, followed by retaining effective employees once they are working for the school district. With student enrollments on the rise and state legislatures mandating smaller class sizes, both U.S. public and private schools are facing an increased demand for additional teachers (Gerald & Hussar, 2003). Couple this with the fact that the U.S. teaching force is, on average, five years older than the average worker in America—and five years closer to retirement age—and it is not surprising that approximately 2.5 million educators need to be hired by 2009 (Hussar, 1999).

Legislation can mandate that teacher qualifications meet specific standards, but it cannot compel highly qualified and highly capable individuals to apply for teaching positions. Consequently, this creates a supply-and-demand problem. By 2013, public enrollment in grades preK–12 in the

United States is projected to increase to 49.7 million students—an increase of 1.5 million students from the estimated enrollment in 2004 (Livingston & Wirt, 2004). While enrollment increases, teachers are leaving the profession and retiring faster than certified new hires can be secured (Ingersoll, 2001). Ingersoll also found that teacher turnover rates (13.2 percent) are higher than the overall national average for worker turnover (11 percent). These teachers may be changing positions within the profession or leaving the profession. Moreover, the aging of the teaching force exacerbates the problem.

It is true that teacher preparation programs currently graduate adequate numbers of teachers and that there are sufficient numbers of certified individuals to meet the needs in most areas. However, teachers may not reside or want to work in the localities that need them. Compounding the supply issue is the fact that approximately 42 percent of newly prepared teachers elect not to teach or are unable to secure teaching positions (Darling-Hammond, 2000a; Dozier & Bertotti, 2000; Edwards, 2000). Henke, Chen, and Geis (2000) reported some of the reasons that graduates who earned their teaching certification gave for not entering the teaching workforce. These reasons included prestige of other professions (2 percent), low pay (7 percent), more lucrative offers (10 percent), and loss of interest in teaching (46 percent).

There seems to be clear evidence that teacher supply and demand, particularly in relation to *high-quality* teacher supply, poses a significant challenge for improving U.S. schools. Clearly, the impact teachers have is measurable and pays dividends beyond what is easily seen. Borrowing the format from a familiar credit card commercial, consider this: cost of a new school—$45 million; cost of a school lunch—$1.75; cost of an effective teacher—priceless!

Tools in the Teacher Selection Process

As illustrated in Figure I, teacher selection is a hierarchical process. Our focus is the two middle sections: the interviews that provide an in-depth opportunity to learn more about an applicant. The Teacher Quality Index is a value-added approach to gathering this information; as such, it does not ask interviewees about information that can be obtained from the employment application (the initial means of evaluation, the focus of which should be to determine if the applicant has the minimum qualifications for the position). Rather, the TQI interview protocol focuses on asking qualified applicants to expand on their abilities, skills, and experiences in an initial screening interview and, later, in a more in-depth building-level interview. The applicant pool is narrowed significantly as successful applicants advance up the pyramid toward the point of final selection.

Within school systems challenged to fill teacher positions, identifying ways to evaluate applicants efficiently and in a value-added manner will enhance the selection process. By developing a systematic way to gather data about candidates for a teaching position, school personnel can work smarter by not duplicating the efforts of others. And in the final analysis,

FIGURE I
The Hierarchical Process of Teacher Selection

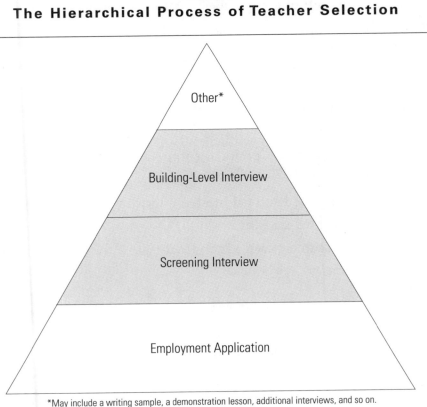

*May include a writing sample, a demonstration lesson, additional interviews, and so on.

we hope they can enhance the predictability of their hires in terms of teacher quality.

Overview of the Book

This book provides concise background information on both interviewing and teacher effectiveness. It presents a research-based approach to teacher selection, and provides and discusses the two-part TQI interview protocol, which is provided in five forms on the accompanying CD-ROM.

The TQI protocol integrates research regarding how to conduct a good interview with research on what constitutes an effective teacher. Selection of high-quality teachers is complex: it is influenced by factors identified in applied psychology, such as interview structure and the phrasing of question prompts, and it draws on effective teacher research. The questions within the TQI are job-related and thus within the legal bounds of interviewing guidelines. Additionally, the TQI protocol is designed to offer a systematic application of the qualities of effective teachers to the selection process. In summary, the Teacher Quality Index

- Blends research on effective teaching with research on effective interviewing.
- Encourages the asking of interview questions that are legally permissible and job relevant.
- Draws from interview protocol components found in applied psychology literature.
- Uses research-based and field-tested interview questions aligned with the qualities of effective teaching.
- Provides research-based and field-tested rubrics to evaluate interviewee responses.

In the final analysis, using the research to strengthen the selection process gives educational leaders a valuable tool to assist them in identifying the applicants who are most likely to become the effective teachers our students need.

PART I

FOUNDATIONS

OF THE

TEACHER QUALITY INDEX

Teacher Quality and Teacher Selection

Teacher *recruitment* is the process of providing an adequate number of quality applicants. Teacher *selection* is the process of choosing only high-quality employees from among the assembled applicants. Hiring, supporting, and sustaining effective teachers is one of the most important responsibilities of school leaders, perhaps *the* most important responsibility. If we believe that teaching and learning are the core of schooling, then we also understand why good teacher selection is absolutely indispensable to high-achieving schools. And for those of us in the United States, identifying and selecting highly qualified individuals to facilitate learning in a productive and academically enriching classroom environment is integral to satisfying the need for capable teachers and fulfilling the requirements of No Child Left Behind.

An examination of the historical context of teacher effectiveness reveals that concern about capable teachers is not a new development. Studies on the qualities of effective teachers in the 1920s focused on personality traits. Today, such studies focus on teaching methods, behavior toward student learning, mastery of competencies, professional decision making, and interaction of pedagological and subject area knowledge (Lederman & Niess, 2001). Of the various conceptual lenses that can be used to consider teacher quality, accountability is the most prominent—meaning the focus tends to be teacher competence and the importance of providing evidence of effectiveness (Yin & Kwok, 1999). And to consider teacher effectiveness, we need to address the following issues:

- The quality indicators of effective teachers
- The connection between teacher quality and teacher selection
- The importance of connecting teacher quality to teacher selection

The Quality Indicators of Effective Teachers

The term "teacher effectiveness"—some definitions of which can be seen in Figure 1.1—is broadly used to identify attributes of what constitutes a good teacher, but it is also dependent upon who is considering the concept. As we use the term throughout this book, *teacher effectiveness* is a set of experiences, traits, behaviors, and dispositions that are typically evident in effective teachers. Words such as *ideal, analytical, dutiful, competent, expert, reflective, satisfying, diversity-responsible,* and *respectful* have been used to describe good teachers (Cruickshank & Haefele, 2001). As demonstrated by this range of adjectives, "There is surprisingly little consensus on how to define a qualified teacher" (Ingersoll, 2001, p. 42).

No Child Left Behind has established a working definition of a qualified teacher as a teacher who is certified in the area in which he or she is

---

FIGURE 1.1
Definitions of Teacher Effectiveness

---

teach•er ef•fec•tive•ness   \'tē-chər i-'fek-tiv-nəs\ *n*

1. A loosely defined concept (Stronge, 2002) that is influenced by individuals' perspectives on what characteristics should be highlighted (Yin & Kwok, 1999).

2. The idea that a teacher cares about students as individuals and communicates that ethic by creating thoughtfully planned, executed, and assessed instructional opportunities in a productive classroom environment in an effort to increase the achievement of each student (Collinson, Killeavy, & Stephenson, 1999).

3. A measure of the academic growth demonstrated by students during the year spent in a teacher's classroom (Sanders & Horn, 1998; Stronge, Tucker, & Ward, 2003).

teaching. Yet there are other measures of quality to consider beyond the federal guidelines, including student achievement, stakeholders' perspectives, and performance ratings. Teacher effectiveness is like beauty; it is often in the eye of the beholder when people recall a special teacher. In doing so, former students often use words like *caring, intelligent, fair, funny, competent,* and *understanding.* Combining what we know from experience with research findings helps to identify integral components that are common in most effective teachers. One way to synthesize the extant research on key attributes, behaviors, and dispositions of effective teachers is to consider six domains—or areas—of teacher effectiveness described by Stronge (2002) in the ASCD publication *Qualities of Effective Teachers:*

- Prerequisites of effective teaching
- The teacher as a person (i.e., personal attributes)
- Classroom management and organization
- Planning for instruction
- Implementing instruction (i.e., instructional delivery)
- Monitoring student progress and potential (i.e., student assessment and student expectations)

Let's examine each of the six areas.

Prerequisites of Effective Teaching

Prerequisites are attributes teachers bring with them to the classroom. Included among key prerequisite qualities are verbal ability, content knowledge, education coursework, teacher certification, and teaching experience.

Verbal Ability. Teachers make connections with their students through words and actions. A teacher's verbal ability has a positive effect on student achievement, as the ability to communicate content knowledge and belief in students is vital to teaching and learning (Darling-Hammond, 2000b; Haberman, 1995b; Hanushek, 1971).

Content Knowledge. A California study found that mathematics teachers who majored or minored in mathematics had students with higher test scores on the Stanford 9 Achievement Test (Fetler, 1999). The benefit of content-area preparation may be due to an intrinsic interest. Wenglinsky (2000) found that teachers with a major or minor in a subject are more likely to attend professional development offerings in that area and, subsequently, incorporate what they learn into instruction.

Education Coursework. In a study of 266 student teachers, educational coursework was a stronger predictor of student teaching performance than grade point average or National Teacher Exam specialty scores (Ferguson & Womack, 1993). Based on these findings, the authors wrote that increasing subject matter coursework and decreasing pedagogical work would be counterproductive, as there is a link between student achievement and teacher education coursework.

Teacher Certification. Teachers assigned to the area in which they are certified have been found to have more influence on student learning than uncertified teachers (Darling-Hammond, 2000b; Darling-Hammond, Berry, & Thoreson, 2001; Goldhaber & Brewer, 2000; Hawk, Coble, & Swanson, 1985; Laczko-Kerr & Berliner, 2002). For example, in a study comparing certified teachers who were licensed to teach mathematics with those licensed in another area, students taught by teachers instructing in their licensed field had higher levels of achievement (Hawk et al., 1985).

Teaching Experience. Experienced teachers have increased depth of understanding of the content and how to teach and apply it (Covino & Iwanicki, 1996). Additionally, experienced teachers are more effective with students due to their use of a wider variety of strategies (Glass, 2001). One study found that "schools with more experienced and more highly educated mathematics teachers tended to have higher achieving students" (Fetler, 1999, p. 9). This quality indicator does not necessarily mean that more years are better. Based on data from the Tennessee Value-Added Assessment System, Sanders and Rivers (1996) found that teachers' effectiveness increased through the first seven years of teaching and became flat by around year 10. (Note: The minimal teaching experience in Sanders' original work was three years.)

The Teacher as a Person

If students are to learn, they need to feel comfortable in their instructional environment. In that respect, the personal connection that an educator makes with students assists in creating a trusting and respectful relationship (Marzano, Pickering, & McTighe, 1993; McBer, 2000). The ability to relate to students and convey a sense that they are valued and that the teacher wants them to be there is vital (Haberman, 1995a). Effective teachers have been described as caring, enthusiastic, motivated, fair, respectful, reflective, and dedicated individuals with a sense of humor who interact well with students and colleagues (Black & Howard-Jones, 2000; Delaney, 1954; National Association of Secondary School Principals [NASSP], 1997; Peart & Campbell, 1999). In brief, teachers' effect on student learning is increased when students are taught by well-prepared professionals who integrate their knowledge of instruction with a deep sense of caring about the individual students they teach. As Sizer (1999) puts it, "We cannot teach students well if we do not know them well" (p. 6).

Classroom Management and Organization

Classroom management and organization encompass skills and approaches teachers use to establish and maintain a safe, orderly, and productive learning environment. There are fewer disruptions and off-task behaviors in effective teachers' classrooms (Stronge et al., 2003). Effective teachers cultivate a positive classroom environment for their students by working with students to ensure that routines, procedures, and expectations are clear; additionally, these teachers take more time at the start of the school year to work with students on creating a positive class climate where individuals are treated with respect and fairness (Covino & Iwanicki, 1996; Emmer, Evertson, & Anderson, 1980; Hoy & Hoy, 2003; Shellard & Protheroe, 2000). They actively teach students their roles, offer clear explanations and directions, rehearse expectations with students, and then give students opportunities to be successful in meeting those expectations (Covino & Iwanicki, 1996; Emmer et al., 1980).

When a discipline issue occurs, effective teachers are not thinking about what to do; they are responding in a predictable manner to the student behavior. In establishing a productive learning environment, effective teachers are recapturing instructional time that is often lost in administrative activities, discipline, and transitions (Hoy & Hoy, 2003). They remain actively involved in students' learning in an organized and positive classroom, as an organized and positive environment is associated with higher achievement gains (Education USA Special Report, n.d.).

Planning for Instruction

The area of planning for instruction offers insights into how effective teachers prioritize and organize instruction, allocate time, and set high expectations for student achievement and behavior. Effective teachers have knowledge about their content area, common student misconceptions, and available resources to use in the classroom (Buttram & Waters, 1997). They possess a deep understanding of the subject matter that facilitates their planning and instructional delivery (Rowan, Chiang, & Miller, 1997). Furthermore, they know how the curriculum relates to the content within the educational landscape (Educational Review Office, 1998). Additionally, they review instructional standards to guide decision making (Buttram & Waters, 1997). These teachers use long-range planning to map where instruction will go in combination with alignment of the curriculum to state and local standards (McEwan, 2001; Walker, 1998). They identify appropriate intended learning outcomes for their students and develop means to assess students on these outcomes during the planning process (Gronlund, 2003; Marzano et al., 1993).

An effective teacher plans for instruction by considering the overarching themes that can be addressed through "big questions" in particular units of study to provide clear and focused instruction in the classroom (Cotton, 2000; Johnson, 1997; McBer, 2000). The teacher incorporates a variety of instructional strategies and resources to facilitate learning and differentiate for student needs (Cunningham & Allington, 1999; Emmer et al., 1980; Mason, Schroeter, Combs, & Washington, 1992; McBer, 2000).

Implementing Instruction

The area of implementing instruction speaks to the nuts and bolts of what occurs in the classroom. Obviously, the way a teacher presents material influences how and how well a student learns it. Teaching is a complex task in which educators must determine the means to instruct students on the essential knowledge and skills to promote the acquisition of new knowledge and abilities (Langer, 2001). Effective teachers expect more from students and this, in turn, raises students' own expectations for success (Entwisle & Webster, 1973; Mason et al., 1992). They provide instruction in which students are actively engaged in minds-on and hands-on activities as they seek to construct meaning from the content while being supported by the teacher (Cunningham & Allington, 1999; Good & Brophy, 1997; Shellard & Protheroe, 2000; Wang, Haertel, & Walberg, 1994). The teacher is actively involved throughout the lesson, providing additional detail and monitoring and adjusting based on student feedback (Education USA Special Report, n.d.; Panasuk, Stone, & Todd, 2002).

Effective teachers know how to use instructional techniques, such as mastery learning and cooperative learning. When used appropriately, these strategies can result in student achievement that is at least one standard deviation higher than that of students taught without the use of the strategies (Bloom, 1984). Effective teachers use technology during instruction to offer more individualized student attention, to provide hands-on experiences, and to shift the focus from the teacher to the student (Dickson & Irving, 2002; Holahan, Jurkat, & Friedman, 2000). These educators also use the students' prior knowledge as a starting point with hands-on, inquiry-based approaches to facilitate increased levels of learning (Covino & Iwanicki, 1996). Furthermore, effective teachers use questioning effectively. They not only ask questions, but also teach students how to ask quality questions themselves with appropriate follow-ups for prompting, redirection, and clarification (Covino & Iwanicki, 1996). Instructional strategies are like transportation vehicles: there are many different types one can use to get to the destination. In the final analysis, effective delivery of instruction is a complex process full of decisions, deviations from the original lesson plan, and responses to student inquiry.

Monitoring Student Progress and Potential

The area of monitoring student progress and potential focuses on how a teacher knows that students have acquired knowledge and skills in a manner that allows pupils to demonstrate academic success. Effective teachers monitor student learning through a variety of informal and formal assessments and offer timely feedback to students (Cotton, 2000; Good & Brophy, 1997; Peart & Campbell, 1999). They check for student understanding throughout a lesson and adjust instruction based on the feedback (Guskey, 1996). These educators align assignments given to students, such as homework and in-class activities, with the intended learning outcomes so they are meaningful to students in developing or reinforcing a concept and meaningful to teachers in analyzing the process and products (Cruickshank & Haefele, 2001). Effective teachers review progress over time using an accumulated body of work, such as a portfolio (Haertel, 1999).

The analysis of student assessment data informs effective teachers about the degree to which students have acquired specific understandings and skills, and guides them in setting instructional goals (Cruickshank & Haefele, 2001; Gronlund, 2003). As teachers analyze student progress, they keep students informed through timely and regular targeted feedback that can help students improve and be more successful in future work (Cotton, 2000; Hoy & Hoy, 2003; Marzano, Norford, Paynter, Pickering, & Gaddy, 2001; Walberg, 1984).

The Connection Between Teacher Quality and Teacher Selection

Although research studies seek to isolate and identify specific characteristics of effective teaching, it is the sum of all the factors that makes a teacher effective. For example, high-quality teachers combine instructional strategies with clearly focused goals and high expectations for both behavior and learning in order to promote student achievement (Cotton, 2000; Johnson, 1997; Marzano et al., 1993; Mason et al., 1992; McBer, 2000; Peart & Campbell, 1999; Shellard & Protheroe, 2000). Thus, while possessing one or even several of the teacher effectiveness quality indicators is not sufficient evidence that an applicant will be an effective teacher, it is a research-informed method designed to increase the likelihood of selecting the best teacher applicants.

The interview is an opportunity to integrate all the different sources of information about a candidate (Castetter, 1996). If interviewers are aware of teacher quality indicators, they will have a toolkit of items that are likely to be indicative of teacher effectiveness. Along with other job-relevant information collected in the selection process—for example, writing samples, portfolios, or observations of demonstration lessons—such indicators allow us to be better informed about what to look for in an applicant and, consequently, more skilled at making research-informed hiring decisions.

A critical issue for school leaders charged with making hiring decisions is how best to capture the desired teacher effectiveness qualities in the review of employment applications and, subsequently, in employment interviews. One way to do this is by asking questions that are explicitly linked to quality indicators and using a rubric that clarifies essential evidence of each indicator to ensure consistent response assessment. It is for this purpose that the Teacher Quality Index was developed. While the methodology and use of the TQI is presented in detail later, Figure 1.2 offers a summary of how we have connected the research on qualities of effective teachers to the interview process.

The Importance of Connecting Teacher Quality to Teacher Selection

Every student deserves a high-quality teacher. In today's K–12 environment, few students are afforded the opportunity to pick their own teachers. Parents' influence is typically minimal, at best. It is largely administrators

FIGURE 1.2

The Qualities of Effective Teachers and the Teacher Quality Index

Quality Domains	Quality Indicators	Employment Application	TQI Protocol	
			Screening Interview	Building-Level Interview
Prerequisites of Effective Teaching	Verbal ability	◆	◆	◆
	Content knowledge	◆	◆	◆
	Knowledge of teaching and learning	◆		
	Certification status	◆	◆	◆
	Teaching experience	◆		
Personal Characteristics	Caring			◆
	Fairness and respect			◆
	Interaction with students			◆
	Enthusiasm		◆	
	Motivation			◆
	Dedication to teaching	◆		
	Reflective practice			◆
Classroom Management	Classroom management			◆
	Organization			◆
	Student discipline		◆	◆
Planning for Instruction	Importance of instruction			◆
	Time allocation		◆	
	Teacher expectations		◆	
	Instructional planning			◆
Instructional Delivery	Instructional strategies		◆	◆
	Content and expectations		◆	
	Complexity			◆
	Questioning			◆
	Student engagement		◆	◆
Assessment	Homework			◆
	Monitoring of student progress		◆	◆
	Response to student needs and abilities		◆	◆

who select students' teachers and make class schedules. Therefore, it is incumbent upon everyone involved in the teacher selection process to make the best possible selection. Although some school systems have the necessary resources to permit observation of teacher applicants in an instructional setting, for many, the teacher selection process is often grounded in the application, with its related documents (e.g., résumé, letters of recommendation, Praxis scores) and the selection interview. What guides these all-important impressions and hiring decisions? How do we know that from a pool of applicants, we've selected the best?

By looking for research-based qualities of effective teachers during the selection process, we increase the likelihood of selecting the best teacher applicants. The typical teacher selection process asks for a plethora of information; we just need to refine our methods of interpreting this information through an effectiveness lens. Research-based qualities of effective teachers can offer decision makers a means to ground what they look for in applications, on résumés, and during interviews. Thus, a well-constructed selection process should create a situation where teachers are selected based on a multitude of factors that ultimately influence student achievement.

In his book *Good to Great* (2001), Jim Collins states, "when in doubt, don't hire—keep looking" (p. 54). The question to consider, however, is how we distinguish high-quality applicants from less-than-high-quality applicants. Moreover, how do we know a good teacher when we see one? What we are really aiming for in teacher selection is *predictive validity*—that is, the ability to use the information available about candidates to make hiring decisions that result in capable and committed teachers. In the final analysis for the teacher selection process, hiring an effective teacher is game, set, and match. Unless we do, in fact, hire quality teachers, we all lose as our schools fail and children suffer.

2

Maximizing the Benefits of Face-to-Face Interviews

The term *selection* suggests that the individuals who make decisions have the tools they need to gather material to make informed choices. The interview comes second only to the employment application in terms of being the most commonly used way to evaluate applicants (Schmidt & Rader, 1999). In making the actual hiring decision, business organizations use interviews the vast majority of the time (Delaney, 1954; Dessler, 1997). More specific to educators' purposes, school administrators use interviews at least 85 percent of the time (Emley & Ebmeier, 1997). School district personnel use various types of interview formats, including telephone, face-to-face, and online interviews. Pros and cons of these formats are addressed in Figure 2.1.

This chapter emphasizes the ways and means of conducting reliable and valid face-to-face interviews. Given the importance of the employment interview in the teacher hiring process, we consider the following issues:

- The history of the employment interview
- The advantages and disadvantages of interviews
- Influences on interview outcomes
- Differentiating factors for success
- Improving teacher selection through better interviewing

The History of the Employment Interview

In 1884, an English newspaper reported, "Interviewing is an instance of the division of labour. . . . The interviewee supplies the matter, the interviewer

FIGURE 2.1
Employment Interview Formats

Interview Format	Purpose	Description	Advantages(s)	Disadvantage(s)
Computer/Online	Screening	Can be designed to eliminate unqualified applicants, assess computer skills, and record reaction time/response to stimulus	Collects information and stores it in a database for searches; saves time and money	Is biased against individuals who are not adept with a computer or information technology
Impromptu Face to Face	Screening	Occurs at job fairs, recruitment parties, and in short interviews with a gatekeeper who decides if the candidate is viable	Reduces the interview load on administrators	Has a first impression bias; is of short duration
Telephone	Screening	Designed to eliminate unqualified applicants	Collects information on skills; saves time and money	Relies on the judgment of one person
Group Interview	Selection	Pairs several interviewers with several job candidates	Views interaction; collects input and ratings from several interviewers	May not allow interviewers to get to know one single candidate well
Panel/Committee	Selection	Occurs with two or more interviewers asking job-related questions, often in a structured interview format	Lets those who will be working with the candidate know what the individual has to offer; lessens Equal Employment Opportunity Commission exposure	Is affected by candidate's comfort level and the skill of the interviewer(s)
Proficiency	Selection	Checks the candidate's ability to perform tasks such as speaking a foreign language or teaching a sample lesson	Sample performance demonstrates what may occur on the job	There may be no correlation between showing a skill and using it in a classroom*
Structured	Selection	Questions take a variety of formats (experience-based, situational, informational); in general, all questions are asked of each candidate in either a one-on-one or panel setup	Encourages active listening by interviewer(s); is more predictive of job performance when valid questions are used	Does not give much feedback to the candidate; depending on the format, follow-up questions may not work

*If performance is evaluated with actual students, this bias is not an issue.

the form" (cited in Edenborough, 1999, p. 16). Interviewing has evolved as a way to get more information about an applicant than the basic information revealed on the job application. It "is the most readily available way of taking account, not merely of the facts of the candidate's career, but of those attitudes, interests . . . that may be supremely important for his subsequent success in the work for which he is being considered" (Anstey & Mercer, 1956, p. 7).

Researchers have been conducting studies for over a century to determine best practices for interviewing (see Figure 2.2). The studies have dissected the various factors that influence an interview, such as legal issues, predictor variables, protocol, structure and questioning. Meta-analysis studies began to emerge near the end of the 20th century. The current research on interviewing shows a trend toward refining the interview process to make it a more valid and reliable tool that is less susceptible to personal interpretation and bias.

FIGURE 2.2
Developments in Interviewing

1920s	1940s	1960s	1970s	1980s	1990s	2000+

Focus on discerning good applicants from bad

Investigation into the role of the interviewer

Scrutiny of interview structures

Further development of computer-assisted interview technologies

Interviews used to match soldiers with jobs

Exploration of the sources of bias

Comparison of question formats

Studies found that using interviews was more reliable than random assignment to positions

Created using information from Eder & Harris, 1999.

The Advantages and Disadvantages of Interviews

Do interviews always work? The definitive answer: yes and no! Interviews can be—and have proven to be—an excellent tool for decision makers to use in the hiring process. However, unless developed along solid, research-based design principles and then implemented with fidelity, the interview is no general prescription for success. Thus, it might be prudent to consider the inherent pros and cons of the interview, as outlined in Figure 2.3.

Educators are adept at recognizing potential and adapting ideas to better serve students. The TQI interview protocol we will detail later was developed from research conducted in other fields.

FIGURE 2.3
Advantages and Disadvantages of Interviewing

Advantages

- May produce in-depth data not obtainable from an application
- Provides a forum for asking questions that require lengthy responses
- Is flexible and adaptable (with certain parameters) to the situation
- May result in more accurate and honest responses because the interviewer can ask for clarification
- Allows for probing with follow-up questions to incomplete or unclear responses
- Provides an opportunity to hear how an applicant communicates
- Offers interviewers a glimpse of how an applicant interacts with others
- Gives an applicant a forum to ask questions
- Lets an applicant "feel out" the organization by meeting representatives of the school (e.g., members of the interview team) during the interview

Disadvantages

- Is expensive in terms of personnel hours
- Is time consuming when compared to a review of applications or testing data
- Involves fewer candidates being reviewed compared with other screening devices (e.g., applications)
- Requires a variety of communication and interpersonal skills
- Is subject to bias:
  - An applicant's response may be positively or negatively affected by a personal reaction to the interviewer
  - An interviewer's first impression may be influenced by an applicant's appearance or initial interaction

---

Influences on Interview Outcomes

The purpose of the employment interview is to exchange information so that the interviewer can determine if a candidate is a good fit for a given position. Yet many factors complicate this rather straightforward purpose. For example, the applicant may be nervous. The interviewer might have conducted several interviews before meeting the applicant and may be tired or already have a "favorite" in mind. First impressions may cloud the interviewer's judgment. For all these reasons and more, the validity (i.e., appropriateness) and reliability (i.e., consistency) of interview-based selection decisions may be highly variable due to influences of several factors.

Accountability. If interviewers are held accountable for *how* they conduct interviews, then their recall of details relating to the applicant is better than if interviewers are accountable only for the outcome of the interview (Brtek & Motowidlo, 2002).

Halo Effect. Interviewers may be influenced by the strength of a previous response to a question when assessing a subsequent question. Using a rating strategy reduces the halo effect by focusing the interviewer on each question (Kiker & Motowidlo, 1998).

Interviewer Training. When interviewers receive training on how to collect job-related information during an interview, they are more effective (Stevens, 1998).

Note Taking. When interviewers voluntarily take notes, their recall of interview-related information is better than if they cannot take notes (Burnett, Fan, Motowidlo, & DeGroot, 1998; Macan & Dipboye, 1994; Middendorf & Macan, 2002).

Personal Interactions. Interviewees may use soft tactics such as ingratiation to make a positive connection with interviewers (Ellis, West, Ryan, & DeShon, 2002; McFarland, Ryan, & Kriska, 2002).

Question Format. The way an interview question is phrased influences the type of information that is gathered. Prompts asking candidates about hypothetical situations result in more consistent ratings than ones asking about opinions or facts (Maurer & Fay, 1988). However, experience-based questions, which ask about actual performance, are more predictive of future job performance than situational questions (Huffcutt, Weekley, Wiesner, DeGroot, & Jones, 2001; Pulakos & Schmitt, 1995; Schmidt & Rader, 1999).

Scoring Method. The use of a scoring mechanism (e.g., rankings, rubrics) is likely to reduce errors in the interview process (Pulakos, Schmitt, Whitney, & Smith, 1996). Rating scales may reduce bias and enhance interviewers' consistency of judgments about candidates' responses (Campion, Palmer, & Campion, 1997).

Structure. A highly structured interview emphasizes job-related constructs, while a less structured interview is better at gathering information about the interviewee as a person (Huffcutt, Conway, Roth, & Stone, 2001). Generally, the structured interview is more valid than its unstructured counterpart (McDaniel, Whetzel, Schmidt, & Maurer, 1994).

Differentiating Factors for Success

In designing a teacher-selection interview protocol, specific consideration should be given to the properties of the interview that research has shown to have greater value. Structured interviews, question format, and rating scales are three mechanisms that enhance the likelihood of an interviewer getting the necessary information and evaluating it to make the best hiring decision.

Structured Interviews

As noted, there are two main types of selection interviews: unstructured and structured. Unstructured interviews tend to emphasize background credentials, personality, and general mental ability. Structured interviews consist of questions related to applied mental skills, direct job knowledge, applied social skills, and organizational fit. They tend to be better predictors of on-the-job success than unstructured interviews (Huffcutt, Conway, Roth, & Stone, 2001).

Common issues that can be considered for structured interviews in education include the teacher's relationship with students, colleagues, and parents; knowledge of instructional techniques and their applications; and general background information (Pawlas, 1995). To increase the validity of the structured interview, all questions should be based on job-related criteria, have anchored rating scales, and use multiple trained interviewers (Campion et al., 1997; Castetter, 1996). This standardized format helps ensure that each candidate responds to the same set of questions and is rated in a common fashion.

Question Format

There is both an art and a science to interview questioning. The way a prompt is phrased predetermines the type of response that will be given. Figure 2.4 presents three question formats, their purposes, and a sample prompt. Which format do you think would be best for getting information about an applicant?

FIGURE 2.4
Types of Interview Questions

Question Type	Description	Sample Prompt
Informational	Candidates are prompted to elaborate on application or résumé information or to recount what they know (e.g., facts, readings)	"What makes a positive and productive classroom climate?"
Situational	Candidates are prompted to explain how they would handle certain hypothetical situations	"School is starting in a week, and you have just received your class list. Another teacher tells you that you have several challenging students assigned to your class. What would you do to ensure that you will foster a positive and productive classroom climate?"
Experience-Based	Candidates are prompted to discuss past performance in a specific case	"Share with me what you do to foster a positive and productive classroom climate."

The *informational* question format asks applicants to tell the interviewer what they know, not specifically what they do. The *situational* question format provides all candidates with the same starting point and lets them determine the outcome. However, research has shown that responses to situational questions often relate more to job knowledge than to performance (Conway & Peneno, 1999). The *experience-based* question requires that applicants tell what they actually can do or have done.

So what question format is best in an interview? The short answer is that experience-based questions tend to be best (see, for example, Huffcutt et al., 2001), and situational questions are better than informational questions (Maurer & Fay, 1988). If you want to know about future performance, ask what the person has done in the past.

Pulakos and Schmitt (1995) considered the predictive validity of experience-based and situational structured interviews with a sample of 216 government employees who had at least three years of work experience and a college degree. The authors trained interviewers to conduct both kinds of interviews in a panel setup with randomly assigned candidates. When the panel's composite rating was compared to the candidate's supervisor's performance rating, only the experience-based interview correlated with actual job performance. Thus, experience-based interviewing was the better predictor of job performance.

In applying this research to teacher selection, one would surmise that experience-based questions would do a better job than other question formats at soliciting information about past performance in the classroom. This makes sense for experienced teachers, but what about novices with limited classroom experience? Would situational questions level the playing field by giving everyone a common baseline? A team of researchers investigated whether a relationship existed between interview ratings and supervisors' performance ratings of trainees who had not yet assumed their job responsibilities. In the interviews, trainees were asked a series of questions that were phrased using either a situational or an experienced-based format. The researchers found that interview ratings for the group in which trainees were asked about their experiences significantly correlated with the performance ratings, whereas the ratings for the group asked situational questions did not (Huffcutt et al., 2001). The interviewees were more effective at conveying information about their performance when given an experience-based question than when they were given a hypothetical situation—even when they were novices.

The experience-based question format may challenge interviewees. As part of the interviewer's introduction to the interviewee, it may be helpful to share the interview format in advance of the interview. Let the interviewee know the interviewer wants to learn about how the interviewee has performed in the past. For individuals new to the teaching profession or returning after an extended hiatus, the interviewer might prompt the interviewees to give examples from other situations. In the case of the sample experience-based question in Figure 2.4 ("Share with me what you do to foster a positive and productive classroom climate."), a newly minted teacher might discuss how he created a positive environment for an incoming fraternity pledge class. A career switcher might explain how she got to know each of her employees and empowered them to have ownership in the office environment. A returning teacher might relate an example of volunteer work.

Rating Scales

The use of a scoring guide grounds interviewers so that they use the same criteria to evaluate responses. As we well know, one person's "excellent" may be another person's "good." Using a common scale with behavioral examples can enhance consistency. A well-developed scoring guide specifies points for good, average, and poor answers (Eder & Harris, 1999). The use of such a scale is assumed to enhance reliability by reducing subjectivity (Campion et al., 1997).

Improving Teacher Selection Through Better Interviewing

Despite longstanding criticism of interviews' validity, they remain the second most commonly used tool for teacher hiring. Research has found that interviews are vital to establishing an organizational match between the candidates' knowledge, skills, and abilities and the culture and needs of the school system (Eder & Harris, 1999). It seems obvious, then, that interviewers (e.g., administrators, teachers, parents, personnel directors) must be trained to conduct more effective interviews and make the best selections.

Questions

Administrators need to consider what they want in a teacher and ask interview questions that will gather information to help them judge whether the interviewee possesses those qualities. In one study, the actual questions asked by middle school principals ($N = 7$) in a school district were analyzed by tape recording teacher employment interviews (with the permission of the parties involved) to determine the content and type of questions being asked of teacher applicants (Perkins, 1998). A significant number of the questions (43 percent) elicited responses of factual knowledge. A follow-up e-mail questionnaire found that the principals' questions and what the principals said they were looking for did not always align. Each principal asked about credentials, instruction, and classroom management, yet noticeably absent were questions about instructional planning, assessment, and the teacher as a person, all qualities relevant to effective teaching.

Accountability for Interview Decisions

A procedure for assessing applicants' responses to interview questions offers the potential for improving teacher hiring decisions. When schools and classrooms are scrutinized for what makes powerful learning experiences, significant effect sizes are found on a variety of items—ranging from the curriculum to the building—but what makes the greatest impact is the teacher. In practice, teacher job descriptions often focus on the knowledge and skills of the profession, which are easier to evaluate than other attributes of effective teachers. A face-to-face interview provides a forum for school personnel to assess the interviewee's disposition, which is more difficult to discern from a résumé and application (Delaney, 1954; Eder & Harris, 1999). However, the interview is susceptible to errors; for example, effective communicators may appear stronger in an interview where questions isolate specific items, whereas in a classroom, knowledge, skills, and dispositions work in combination. Conversely, an outstanding teacher may seem nervous in an interview and lack the confidence that is predominant in his or her work with students. Therefore, an interview protocol must be sensitive to these concerns and help interviewers triangulate a variety of sources of information to make an informed judgment.

Making the Interview Process Better

School districts' human resource departments are under continual pressure to provide school administrators with a pool of qualified teacher candidates. No Child Left Behind simplifies the process of identifying "highly qualified" teachers: it's primarily a matter of looking at certification. Therefore, the challenge for HR departments is not searching for highly *qualified* teachers, but rather enhancing the likelihood that they are screening for and selecting highly *effective* teachers. The literature on teacher effectiveness and interviewing provides the basis for the Teacher Quality Index interview protocol, which is designed to support interviewers in distinguishing promising teachers from those with less potential to be effective. The TQI protocol asks teacher applicants about their past performance, and the interviewer or interview team uses an anchored rubric to evaluate responses. Figure 2.5 illustrates the alignment of some sample TQI prompts to the qualities of effective teachers.

What is important to note is the distribution of prompts across the range of qualities of effective teachers. It is not an equal distribution; the quality associated with instructional delivery is more heavily weighted. One key feature of the TQI protocol that is different from many published sets of interview question sets is its emphasis on instruction. Classroom management, planning, assessment, and personal characteristics also influence what occurs in the classroom; these factors are represented by multiple questions. Further information on TQI prompts and the interview formats is presented in Chapter 4.

FIGURE 2.5

TQI Prompt Alignment with the Qualities of Effective Teachers

Sample TQI Prompt	Personal Characteristics	Classroom Management	Planning for Instruction	Instructional Delivery	Assessment
1. What do you find most rewarding about teaching?	◆				
2. Tell me what you do with students during the first few weeks you are working with them to establish a positive classroom environment.		◆			
3. Share with me your long- and short-term planning process for instruction.			◆		
4. Describe how you engage students in their learning.				◆	
5. Share with me a time you had difficulty with a particular student's behavior and what you did to address it.		◆			
6. Explain your grading system to me.					◆
7. Think about an instructional unit you have taught. Tell me why you selected particular instructional strategies to teach the curriculum.				◆	
8. Tell me how your assessments accommodate students' learning needs.					◆
9. Give me an example of how you establish and maintain rapport with your students.	◆				
10. Describe how you promote high expectations for student achievement.				◆	
11. How does your use of instructional time demonstrate that learning is students' primary purpose?				◆	
12. How do you use technology as part of your instruction?			◆		
13. Pick a topic in your subject area that is often difficult for students to understand. Tell me what the topic is and how you explain it to students, and share with me directions for an activity you do to help further students' understanding of that topic.				◆	
14. Think about a lesson that did not meet your expectations, despite planning and preparation. Tell me what you considered when planning to readdress the topic with your students and describe how you altered your approach.	◆				

3

Legal Considerations in Teacher Selection

Just as treating others fairly is the right thing to do in our everyday personal lives, it's the right thing to do while evaluating teacher candidates in our professional lives. The latter is also legally required. As Dessler (1997) points out, it makes sense for employers to guarantee fair treatment of employees for several reasons, and one of them is that we live and work in an increasingly litigious environment. Thus, we must take care to conduct all personnel processes and decisions in a fair, ethical, and legal manner. In this chapter, we address the following issues related to legal considerations in teacher selection:

- How U.S. law mandates accountability in teacher selection
- The legal framework for teacher selection
- Federal laws relating to teacher selection
- Components of a fair and legal employment application
- What constitutes a legally defensible interview
- What interview questions can and cannot be asked

How U.S. Law Mandates Accountability in Teacher Selection

In the United States, federal and state legislation concerning accountability and teacher quality has attempted to ensure quality education for the nation's future workforce. School districts must identify, select, and retain high-quality teachers. Local educational agencies must report annual increases in the percentages of highly qualified instructional personnel in school systems to the state (No Child Left Behind Act of 2001).

The U.S. Department of Education has stated that "quality teaching . . . means bringing distinctive life experiences and perspectives to the classroom; providing valuable role models for minority and non-minority students alike; enriching the curriculum, assessment, and school climate; and strengthening connections to parents and communities" (1998, p. 3). The goal of the legal mandates, simply put, is to place an effective teacher in every classroom.

Some states interpret "highly qualified" to mean that teachers must undergo additional training or have a college major in the subject area that they teach, and make these mandatory conditions of obtaining a teaching license. In order to be fully licensed, various states require prospective teachers to pass PRAXIS or other teacher-entry tests at prescribed cut-score levels.

The Legal Framework for Teacher Selection

U.S. public policy concerning personnel processes and decisions has evolved over time to reflect the following fundamental elements for *equal employment opportunity*:

- Potential candidates must be apprised that jobs are available.
- Candidates must be evaluated in terms of characteristics that make a difference between success and failure on the job.
- Employees must be treated equally while on the job.

As Cascio (2003) notes: "Although no law has ever attempted to define precisely the term *discrimination,* in the employment context it can be viewed broadly as the giving of an unfair advantage (or disadvantage) to the members of a particular group in comparison with the members of other groups" (p. 79). Accordingly, employers must ensure that their employment practices—including application forms and interview questions and protocols—adhere to the following requirements.

- *They must be indiscriminant.* The position must be open to all.
- *They must be valid.* Job screening must be relevant to the job, either predictive of success on the job or reflective of actual job requirements.
- *They must be fair.* Employment application requirements and interview questions must relate to the nature of the job.

Equal Employment Opportunity Guidelines stipulate that unfair queries *must* be eliminated. Specifically, this means interviewers may not ask any questions that lead to an adverse impact on employment of identifiable groups, that do not address the requirements of the job or concern a bona fide occupational qualification (BFOQ), or that constitute an invasion of privacy.

Federal Laws Relating to Teacher Selection

Numerous federal laws protect the rights of U.S. citizens, both during the job search process and after hiring.

Selected U.S. Constitution Articles and Amendments

The U.S. Constitution has been interpreted to provide protections against unlawful personnel decisions. Key provisions that are applicable to our discussion of teacher selection include the following:

- *Article I, Section 10.* "No state shall . . . pass any . . . Law impairing the Obligation of Contracts."
- *Amendment I.* "Congress shall make no law respecting an establishment of religion, or prohibiting the free exercise thereof; or abridging the freedom of speech, or of the press, or the right of the people peaceably to assemble, and to petition the Government for a redress of grievances."
- *Amendment XIV, Section 1.* "All persons born or naturalized in the United States and subject to the jurisdiction thereof, are citizens of the United States and of the State wherein they reside. No State shall make or enforce any law which shall abridge the privileges or immunities of citizens

of the United States; nor shall any State deprive any person of life, liberty, or property, without due process of law; nor deny to any person within its jurisdiction the equal protection of the laws."

Thus, contractual issues related to employment, personal freedoms, and the application of those freedoms to state laws have an impact on selection decisions.

Selected Federal Statutes

Until the mid-1960s, employment interviewing and teacher selection were relatively unrestricted in the United States. Key provisions of the Civil Rights Act of 1964—the leading legislation in employment issues—follow:

Civil Rights Act of 1964 (Public Law 88-352), 42 U.S.C.§ 2000e-e-2.
Title VII, Equal Employment Opportunities
§ 2000e-2 Unlawful employment practices. Employer practices.

(a) It shall be an unlawful employment practice for an employer—

(1) to fail or refuse to hire or to discharge any individual, or otherwise to discriminate against any individual with respect to his compensation, terms, conditions, or privileges of employment, because of such individual's race, color, religion, sex, or national origin; or

(2) to limit, segregate, or classify his employees or applicants for employment in any way which would deprive or tend to deprive any individual of employment opportunities or otherwise adversely affect his status as an employee, because of such individual's race, color, religion, sex, or national origin.

As clearly stated in the law itself, the Civil Rights Act of 1964 prohibits discrimination based on race, sex, religion, or national origin. Title VI specifically prohibits discrimination by any program receiving federal funding, and Title VII prohibits discrimination in public sector employment. Additionally, Title VII established the Equal Employment Opportunity Commission to investigate cases of alleged discrimination. Although the list presented in Figure 3.1 is not comprehensive, it does offer a brief review of key federal statutory provisions connected to teacher selection and related employment practices.

FIGURE 3.1
Selected Federal Statutes Related to Employment

Statute	Content
Equal Pay Act, 1963	• Requires equal pay for males and females for comparable jobs • Does not apply under performance-based compensation systems
Age Discrimination in Employment Act (ADEA), 1967	• Prohibits age discrimination • Protects individuals age 40 and above • Applies to all governmental units and private employers of 29 or more individuals • Does not apply when age is a bona fide qualification of employment
Equal Employment Opportunity Act, 1972	• Extends coverage of ADEA to all private employers of 15 or more persons, educational institutions, state and local governments, public and private employment agencies, labor unions with 15 or more members, and joint committees for apprenticeships and training
Rehabilitation Act, 1973	• Prohibits discrimination based on a handicap • Requires reasonable accommodation in the work environment • Requires job-related employment selection criteria • Applies to recipients of federal financial assistance
Americans with Disabilities Act, 1990 (Titles I and V)	• Extends the Rehabilitation Act of 1973 to the private sector and those governmental agencies that receive no federal monies • Makes it unlawful to discriminate against the disabled in any personnel action • Includes protected classes for the following disabilities: cerebral palsy, muscular dystrophy, multiple sclerosis, AIDS, HIV infection, emotional illness, drug addiction, alcoholism, and dyslexia • Requires that the employee must otherwise qualify for the position and must satisfy job requirements • Allows punitive damages (not allowed against school districts) • Establishes requirements for barrier-free buildings • Requires reasonable accommodation to job or work environment except where it creates undue hardship (i.e., is unduly costly, substantial, or disruptive, or alters the fundamental operation of the organization)
Civil Rights Act, 1991	• Allows monetary damages in cases of intentional employment discrimination • Provides right to jury trial • Clarifies adverse impact (unintentional discrimination) obligations • Amends the Civil Rights Act of 1964 to protect workers against intentional discrimination in all aspects of employment • Makes it unlawful to adjust scores on employment-related tests as an affirmative action process
Family and Medical Leave Act, 1993	• Provides workers up to 12 weeks unpaid leave each year for birth, adoption, or foster care of a child within a year of the child's arrival • Provides for leave for care of a spouse, parent, or child with a serious health condition • Provides for leave for an employee's own serious health condition if it prevents him/her from working

Components of a Fair and Legal Employment Application

Because the application is the first step for many school districts when they consider employing a teacher, it is important to consider how this screening tool contributes to the selection process. The application is the most logical place to collect basic information about education, certification, and experience; each of these topics is legally permissible, as they are job related. A less obvious job-related question asks if applicants have been convicted of a violation of law other than minor traffic violations. The question is legally permissible because schools have a duty to protect the students they serve.

Employment applications use a variety of formats to collect basic contact information as well as initial job-related criteria. Although a hiring decision should *not* be made solely on the basis of a school system's employment application, the application is wisely used to try to tease out evidence of effective teaching. Figure 3.2 illustrates how the application can be mined for prerequisite knowledge, skills, and attributes associated with qualities of effective teachers. Using the employment application to identify specific quality indicators allows administrators to make better decisions about which candidates should advance to the interview stage.

What Constitutes a Legally Defensible Interview

While the interview is widely used to screen individuals for their suitability for employment, the process is too often misused. Litigation statistics show that most discrimination cases in which the U.S. Equal Employment Opportunity Commission (EEOC) is involved are linked to violations of Title VII of the Civil Rights Acts of 1964 (Public Law 88-352) and 1991 (Public Law 102-166) [Equal Employment Opportunity Commission, 2002]. Title VII prohibits discrimination on the basis of race, color, religion, sex, or national origin; a statement to this effect often appears on the bottom of employment postings and applications. Other statutes enforced by the EEOC include the

FIGURE 3.2

Finding Prerequisites of Effective Teaching on the Employment Application

Look for	Why	Sources for Additional Information
Certification Status	Certified teachers assigned to teach in their area of certification are more effective than those who are teaching out-of-field or who are not certified	Darling-Hammond, 2000b; Darling-Hammond, Berry, & Thoreson, 2001; Goldhaber & Brewer, 2000; Hawk et al., 1985; Laczko-Kerr & Berliner, 2002; Ross, Cousins, Gadalla, & Hannay, 1999
	No Child Left Behind calls for highly qualified teachers, which can be defined as certified teachers assigned to their areas of certification	No Child Left Behind, 2001
A Major or Minor in the Subject Area to be Taught	A major or minor in the subject an educator teaches is related to higher levels of student achievement	Fetler, 1999
	Teachers who have completed educational coursework are knowledgeable about how students learn and about how to package material for student learning	Berliner, 1986; Scherer, 2001
Education Coursework	Educational coursework is a stronger predictor of teacher effectiveness than grade point average or teacher test scores	Ferguson & Womack, 1993
Teaching Experience	Teaching experience influences teacher effectiveness, particularly in the areas of planning, classroom management, questioning, and reflection	Covino & Iwanicki, 1996; Fetler, 1999; Reynolds, 1992
	Students of experienced teachers often have higher levels of achievement	Fetler, 1999; Glass, 2002; Wenglinsky, 2000
Professional Development	Teachers who have received professional development offerings that relate to the content area or population of students taught have their effectiveness enhanced, resulting in higher levels of student academic success	Camphire, 2001; Cross & Regden, 2002
	Professional development work in technology is an emerging area related to effectiveness	International Society for Technology in Education, n.d.

Americans with Disabilities Act (ADA) of 1990 (Public Law 101-336), the Age Discrimination in Employment Act (ADEA) of 1967 (Public Law 90-202), and the Equal Pay Act (EPA) of 1963 (Public Law 88-38).

The Americans with Disabilities Act prohibits discrimination in the private and public sectors against qualified individuals who have disabilities. Given that some employment positions have physical requirements, employers may specify the types of tasks required to perform the job and ask applicants if they can do them.

Individuals who are over age 40 and seeking employment may not be discriminated against on the basis of age, according to ADEA. Regardless of gender, individuals performing essentially the same work are entitled to the same pay, as stated in the EPA. Of these acts, Title VII, ADA, and ADEA directly affect interviewing.

Young, Rinehart, and Baits (1997) investigated the impact of age in screening for teacher applicants. In two separate studies, information packets were mailed to practicing principals asking them which candidate they would hire for the position of a physical education teacher ($N = 360$) or a physics teacher ($N = 495$). The response rate to each questionnaire was over 60 percent. Principals were given information about two applicants whose qualifications were the same, but the adjectives used to describe them indicated that one was 29 years old and the other was 49. In the case of the physical education teacher, the younger candidate was preferred, which may be an indicator of age discrimination. No significant difference was found in the selection of the physics teacher.

Diligence exercised by employers during the selection process can ward off lawsuits. For example, Williamson, Campion, Malos, Roehling, and Campion (1997) found that employers who have developed standard interview questions, trained their interviewers, and designed and validated the interview process have thought through what occurs in the selection interview and taken steps to ensure that candidates are treated in a legal and ethical manner. In that study of 99 lawsuits (Williamson et al., 1997), judges' rulings focused on the job-relatedness of the interview, such as specific job-related questions and criteria, as opposed to how the interview was conducted. Other studies on legal considerations examine the issue of disparate impact caused by the use of predictor variables (Young et al., 1997).

In an effort to increase the likelihood of good hiring decisions, some institutions use predictor variables, which are factors such as test scores that indicate which applicants have the required skills and knowledge to do the job. These variables should not have adverse effects on any particular demographic group. For example, if applicants for a grocery store cashier's position are given a skills test on recognizing produce, individuals over 40 years of age should be selected at approximately the same rate as their younger counterparts. However, even if a predictor variable is favorable to the majority, it should not be removed from the selection process (De Corte, 1999).

An example of the use of a predictor variable in education is the National Teacher Exam. The U.S. Supreme Court ruled that the use of the exam did not violate Title VII of the Civil Rights Act, even though it disqualified many minority teacher applicants in South Carolina, because the test measured individual achievement on specific subject matter necessary for employment (*United States et al. v. State of South Carolina*, 1977). Other commonly used predictor variables in education include college grade point average and student teacher performance reports for new graduates (Shechtman & Sansbury, 1989). In the final analysis, school districts must use all the best predictor variables at their disposal to select the most qualified candidates to teach students, while at the same time they must be sensitive to any unjustified disparate impact that could exist.

Which Interview Questions Can and Cannot Be Asked

Asking the wrong questions can expose a prospective employer to substantial liability if those questions tread on prohibited territory. Consider the following case in point, cited by Ruiz and Sperow (1997):

> [In 1997] a jury awarded a job applicant $157,500 because the prospective employer asked during the applicant's interview, "What current or past

medical problems might limit your ability to do a job?" Although the company asserted that the applicant was not hired because he was rude, the jury concluded that the interview question was illegal under the Americans with Disabilities Act. (p. 1)

So what *can* we ask? An interview can be used to explore job-relevant issues in depth by posing both basic and follow-up questions. Also, the interview can be a good tool for determining a match between a candidate and the organization. However, generally, any inquiries that were illegal in the employment application process are also illegal in the interview. Even casual chat about the candidate's family can be construed as an impermissible line of inquiry. Thus, interviewers need to make sure that all questions focus on job-related responsibilities.

What Works: Practical Guidelines for Legal Interviews

In an effort to make teacher selection decisions that are balanced and legally defensible, Peterson (2002) offers a very useful summation of good practices to help ensure the legality of hiring practice:

- Seek competent legal advice.
- Keep applicant identities confidential.
- Verify all recruitment materials.
- Do not enumerate too many specifics in job offer letters, lest they be perceived as conditions for employment.
- Do not tell unsuccessful applicants why they were passed over.
- Evaluate your selection program.
- Train and evaluate all newly hired teachers.

What we advocate is protecting the rights of prospective teachers while at the same time allowing the school district to collect needed job-relevant information in order to make good hiring decisions.

Teacher selection is complex, and as the need for more teachers increases in school districts due to teacher turnover, higher enrollment numbers, and teacher retirement, the process by which applicants are selected needs thoughtful attention. Training building-level administrators in what constitutes a fair and legal interview is one step. Adopting an interview protocol that aligns the school's need for effective teachers with the questions asked is another. The final step is to consider selection as part of a cycle in which the extension of a position offer is merely the beginning, after which an administrator can compare how a teacher's performance is reflective of what was seen during his or her interview. The reality is that just as some teachers are more effective than others, some administrators are better than others at discerning in an interview who will be a good or great teacher.

PART II

APPLICATION

OF THE

TEACHER QUALITY INDEX

Interviewing and Identifying the Best Applicants

In most school systems, district-level human resource departments review submitted employment applications and résumés and then conduct a short screening interview with promising applicants to learn more about the applicants' job-related knowledge, skills, and abilities. These interviews may be conducted at job fairs, on the telephone, via video conferencing, online, or face to face. The most qualified applicants are then recommended for building-level interviews, after which hiring decisions are typically made. For this reason, the Teacher Quality Index protocol consists of two parts: one for screening interviews and one for building-level interviews (see Chapter 6).

In this chapter we consider the following topics:

* Factors that influence interview decisions.
* Ways to enhance the effectiveness of interview decisions.
* Research supporting the TQI protocol's core interview questions.
* How to establish a common understanding of interview response quality.
* How to address the challenges that using the TQI protocol may bring about.

Factors that Influence Interview Decisions

Various factors influence the decisions reached after interviews are held. These range from personality clashes to environmental conditions, like an interview room that is too warm or too cool. Figure 4.1 represents the reality in many teacher selection interviews—a bombardment of influences without any filters or guidance. Although many of the terms in the figure are familiar, some elaboration is warranted:

• *Affective characteristics* of the interviewee include the sound of the voice, smile, attractiveness, ability to relate, and a host of otherwise intangible items.

• *Anticipated response* is a source of interviewer bias in which a particular answer is expected.

FIGURE 4.1
Influences on Interview Decisions

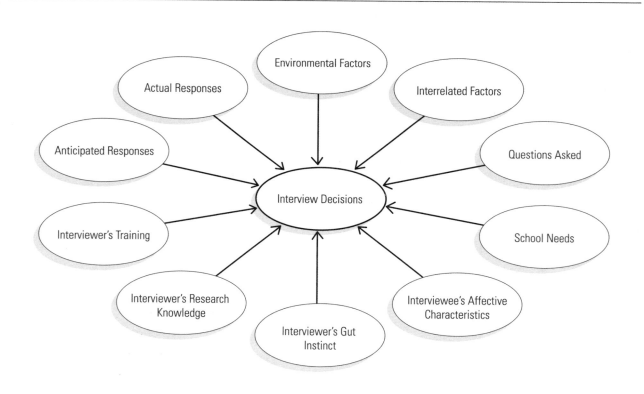

- *Environmental factors* are influences beyond the control of the interviewee or interviewer, such as a fire alarm or room temperature.
- *Gut instinct* is just how the interviewer feels about the interview.
- *Interrelated factors* is a catch-all designation for how factors seem to compound one another at times.
- *Interviewer's research knowledge* is what the interviewer knows about the content and educational practices.
- *Interviewer training* is knowing what are appropriate and inappropriate inquiries and knowing how to ask probing questions that obtain the information needed to make an informed decision.
- *Questions asked* determine the responses given. Accordingly, the question set needs to inquire about a multitude of factors relating to effective teaching. Additionally, the prompts need to be phrased such that interviewees share what they have done, not just their opinions on particular topics.
- *Responses to questions* refers to the quality of the answer in terms of its demonstration of knowledge of the content, students, and teaching.
- *School needs* are those items that are not written on a job description, but do influence how the applicant would work within the school. For example, if an interviewee will be team-teaching, how the personalities of the various teachers on the team would interact with the interviewee's personality is a consideration. Hopefully, an interviewee would not be hired solely because of past experience coaching a sport or sponsoring a particular club. However, if all other professional aspects are equal, the school's need for someone to sponsor an extracurricular activity may put one applicant "over the top."

Figure 4.2 represents what is occurring in the TQI interview protocol, in which both the question sets and scoring rubrics are derived from research on the qualities of effective teachers. It emphasizes decision making through the lens of available research. Note that the protocol still acknowledges the various influences that factor in interview decisions, but these are sidelined in favor of the research-based criteria. For an analogy, think of how fans at a football game can influence the outcome of a game

FIGURE 4.2
Interview Decisions with the Teacher Quality Index

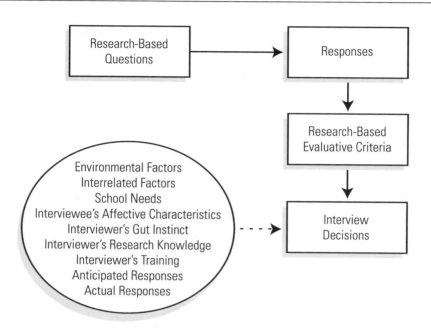

in an intangible way by influencing how the players feel. Still, it's the players actions that ultimately determine who wins or loses.

Ways to Enhance the Effectiveness of Interview Decisions

Integrating the literature on the qualities of effective teachers with what research says works in interviewing is one step toward better interview decisions. The TQI protocol combines what we know makes a difference in interviewing with what we know makes a difference in the classroom. Each of the protocol's components is grounded in the extant research. In both the screening and building-level interviews, applicants are asked a series of questions related to each teacher quality domain. After listening to each response, interviewers assign a rating. At the end of the interview, points are recorded by quality area and then summed for a total value. In the building-level TQI question set, there is an additional section for ordering candidates by rank. Why assign a rank? In a study of interview techniques investigating whether interviewers' ranking of interviewees would match a rank order list of the interviewees based on their previous performance, ranking was found to be productive (Maurer & Lee, 2000). In practical terms, the process of assigning a rank may help interview teams come to consensus more quickly about who the top applicants are. Part II of this book provides the TQI protocol forms and a training document that allows you to compare your rating of sample responses to the composite rating given by a sample of public school principals in the United States.

Although interviewing is often a necessity for building-level administrators as they replace teachers or fill new classroom positions, nearly three-quarters of administrators who participated in a national survey had not received training in how to interview teachers, and most learned to interview from other administrators (Hindman, 2004). This finding presents some potential problems: (1) well-intentioned administrators may unknowingly perpetuate ineffective interview habits; and (2) administrators may not be aware of EEOC guidelines. For example, a qualitative dissertation study reported that principals did not ask the questions that solicited the information they wanted and sometimes asked illegal hiring questions (Perkins, 1998). When employers train their interviewers and use standard protocols, the interview process is more reliable and valid (Williamson et al., 1997).

Training in structured interviewing has been found to improve the reliability and validity of hiring decisions (Dipboye & Gaugler, 1993; Maurer & Fay, 1988). Having administrators trained in effective interviewing practices can result in better decision making, which in turn provides better teachers to students, reduces nonrenewal of teacher contracts for poor performance, and decreases the time and money spent on teacher selection.

For the purposes of introducing the format of TQI question sets, let's depart from teacher selection for a moment. Imagine a 16-year-old boy who is trying to convince his parents that he is ready to get his driver's license. How will his parents determine whether or not he really is prepared—really is ready for the responsibility? What if they had a protocol like the one in Figure 4.3? (Note that each component in this example corresponds to a component of the TQI interview protocol.)

Question. The prompt is phrased so that the 16-year-old needs to respond to it from his perspective and based on his experiences. It is designed to get him to talk about his behavior and motivation.

Sample Quality Indicators. Quality indicators are provided as specific examples of related constructs that could be addressed in responding to the question. They are a means to focus the interviewer on what the interviewee could be expected to say. In the case of a 16-year-old prospective driver, the indicators are items that others may know as good responses to this particular

---

FIGURE 4.3

An Example Interview Protocol

PROMPT: **Tell me why you are ready to get your driver's license.**

Sample Quality Indicators	Notes		
• Successfully completed driver's education course • Collected the paperwork needed to get the license • Responsible/mature in other aspects of life, such as homework, babysitting			
❏ **Unsatisfactory**	❏ **Developing**	❏ **Proficient**	❏ **Exemplary**
"All my friends can drive, and I want to get a car."	"I did not mess up with my learner's permit and now I am old enough."	"Since I finished driver's ed and spent time behind the wheel with you, I think I am ready to help out by driving my sister to soccer by myself."	"I know driving is a big responsibility and I am ready for everything it entails, from helping with car expenses like insurance and gas to watching out for other drivers."

question. (For the TQI protocol, the indicators are based on research on effective teachers.) The indicators are not intended to be seen as the "correct answer"; they are merely samples (Huffcutt, Weekley, Wiesner, DeGroot, & Jones, 2001; Pulakos & Schmitt, 1995; Schmidt & Rader, 1999).

Space for Notes. A note-taking section is provided to record important points. Note taking is not mandatory within the TQI interview protocol. However, two studies conducted by Burnett, Fan, Motowidlo, and DeGroot (1998) underscore that, when given the opportunity to take notes during interviews, interviewers tend to record more information about job performance—what interviewees actually have done or currently do in their jobs—than about other factors, such as leadership, disposition, or behavior. This increases the validity (i.e., appropriateness) of the interview. Additionally, note taking can improve recall about an interviewee and his or her responses (Macan & Dipboye, 1994; Middendorf & Macan, 2002).

A Four-Level Rubric. A rubric creates a common set of guidelines. Each interviewer, based on his or her prior experiences, knowledge, and other factors (such as those identified in Figure 4.2), approaches a question differently in terms of what he or she wants to hear. A scoring rubric defines what is important for a given task (Goodrich, 1996). It also improves an individual's consistency in scoring and reduces subjectivity in group scores (Campion et al., 1997). When multiple interviewers rate interview responses item by item, inter-rater reliability tends to be higher than when reviewers simply provide an overall rating at the end of the interview (Taylor & Small, 2002). For our 16-year-old in the example, if two parents are involved in the decision-making process, both would use the same set of guidelines to determine how ready they think their teenager is to drive.

Research Supporting the TQI Protocol Core Interview Questions

For the Teacher Quality Index, we examined each of the 6 quality domains described in Chapter 1 and identified 14 core qualities. Over the next few pages, we provide sample interview questions designed to encourage applicants to discuss experiences relating to these 14 qualities. Each prompt is succeeded by a few bullets summarizing select research on effective teaching. We include them to illustrate why the interview questions in the TQI protocol can be valuable in helping to distinguish among teacher applicants.

Prerequisites of Effective Teaching

Ideally, the employment application that an interviewee completes prior to the interview is full of information relating to this quality area. Because the application inquires about education, years of experience, and other credentials, the interviewer does not have to cover these topics, and the TQI protocol does not directly ask interviewees to talk about their content knowledge. However, applicants are likely to use content-rich examples when responding to questions about lesson preparation, classroom teaching, or assessment of students. (See, for example, the question for the core quality "Instructional Complexity" on p. 57.) The interviewer's judgment of the interviewee's content knowledge that is shared while responding to specific questions is additional useful information, and the concluding item on both parts of the TQI protocol (screening-level and building-level) asks the interviewer to provide this.

Core Quality: Content Knowledge
Based on the candidate's interview, provide an overall rating of the candidate's knowledge of the content matter.

• Content knowledge enables the integration of essential skills and knowledge (Langer, 2001).

• Teachers with a major or minor in some subjects, like math and science, have students who outperform peers taught by educators without the subject matter background (Wenglinsky, 2000). These educators tend to be certified in their field, resulting in higher levels of achievement on standardized tests (Wenglinsky, 2000). They can convey their enthusiasm, understanding, and knowledge to students.

The Teacher as a Person

When students are asked to describe the teacher who made the biggest impact on them, they often start with personal qualities before talking about subject matter knowledge and what the teacher did in the classroom. Effective teachers feel optimistic about their profession, establish positive relationships with their students, and engage in reflective practice.

Core Quality: Enthusiasm and Motivation

PROMPT: *What do you find most rewarding about the teaching profession?*

• Teachers' enthusiasm for learning and for their content area often influences their students' attitudes toward the subject (Edmonton Public Schools, 1993).

• Collegial school environments have an energy fostered by teachers socializing with each other and building a sense of community (Hoy & Hoy, 2003).

Core Quality: Interactions with Students

PROMPT: *Give me an example of how you establish and maintain a rapport with your students.*

• Effective teachers are friendly and confident, and seek to understand students (Wubbels, Levy, & Brekelmans, 1997).

• Effective teachers use the established relationship as a positive source of influence (Northwest Regional Education Laboratory, 2001).

Core Quality: Reflective Practice

PROMPT: *Think about a lesson that did not meet your expectations, despite planning and preparation. Tell me what you considered when planning to read-dress the topic with your students and describe how you altered your approach.*

• Effective teachers use reflection to align what they believe with what they do (Corcoran & Leahy, 2003).

• Reflection is a regular and routine part of professional practice (Grossman et al., 2000). It may be done alone or with the assistance of others.

Classroom Management and Organization

Classroom management and organization broadly refer to the environment of the classroom: the rules, procedures, and setup that influence how the students operate within the classroom. Depending on the teacher and the students, this environment may be buzzing with the hum of students talking and working on assignments, quiet, or even chaotic, in a worst-case scenario. Elements of effectiveness can even be seen when the teacher is not in the room or visualized as the teacher describes the room without students in it. Yet the true measure of effectiveness is how the teacher and the students work in the environment.

Core Quality: Classroom Management

PROMPT: *Tell me what you do with students during the first few weeks of the school year to establish a positive classroom environment.*

• Effective teachers establish routines, practice rules, and promote ownership of the classroom (Shellard & Protheroe, 2000).

• Effective teachers set a tone through their actions that assures students that the classroom is a safe place to grow both academically and socially. They also create a positive climate so students are excited about learning (Kohn, 1996).

Core Quality: Student Discipline

PROMPT: *Share with me a time you had difficulty with a particular student's behavior and what you did to address it.*

• Effective teachers address concerns in an appropriate, fair, and consistent way (Shellard & Protheroe, 2000; Thomas & Montgomery, 1998).

• Effective teachers may use cuing to indicate what should occur (Education USA Special Report, n.d.).

Planning for Instruction

Planning for instruction refers to all the aspects of planning and preparation that a teacher does before students enter the classroom for an instructional day. In terms of lesson planning, it includes both long- and short-term planning, which typically consists of reviewing state standards, district curriculum, and educational materials (such as textbooks, supplemental resources, and Web sites) and determining what supplies are needed for the class. During this organizational period, teachers are designing the instructional plan. Teachers may gather items or create original instructional materials to support the lesson plan.

Core Quality: Planning

PROMPT: *Share with me your long- and short-term planning process for instruction.*

 • Effective teachers may make long-range plans together in order to mentor teachers new to the grade level or subject area and to gather additional insights from others (Darling-Hammond, 2001).

 • Effective teachers review short-term plans to ensure that they meet students' needs, are appropriately paced, and possess a feedback mechanism (Cruickshank & Haefele, 2001).

Core Quality: Planning for Technology Use

PROMPT: *How do you use technology during your instruction?*

 • Technology can be used to shift focus to a student-centered classroom through the use of hands-on activities and individualized instruction (Dickson & Irving, 2002).

 • Effective teachers plan to use technology as a tool to improve skills such as writing (Rockman et al., 1998).

Note that "technology" is not synonymous with computers; it is a term used to incorporate various types of applications and equipment, from calculators and DVDs to computer applications.

Implementing Instruction

Implementing instruction is perhaps the most public of all the effective teacher qualities. It is where the behind-the-scenes work of planning comes to fruition, and the assessment that follows continues the cycle of instruction. This is the "teacher teaching," through lecturing, directing students as they acquire new skill sets, facilitating an investigation, or by engaging in a host of other instructional formats.

Core Quality: Student Engagement

PROMPT: *Describe how you engage students in their learning.*

• Students who are engaged in their learning are actively participating in the process. To encourage student engagement, effective teachers have been found to provide open-ended performance assignments that enable students to demonstrate what they know (Eisner, 1999).

• Effective teachers use student-centered instruction as a motivator for students (Johnson, 1997).

Core Quality: Instructional Strategies

PROMPT: *Think about a unit you taught. Tell me why you selected particular instructional strategies to teach the curriculum.*

• Instructional strategies are a means to reaching the intended learning outcomes. Effective teachers recognize that some strategies work better than others in particular situations or with certain students, so they use a variety of strategies (Darling-Hammond, 2001; Educational Review Office, 1998).

• Cooperative learning is an instructional strategy commonly used to involve students and enhance higher-order thinking skills (Shellard & Protheroe, 2000).

• Hands-on learning results in students achieving at higher levels than peers taught without manipulatives or simulations (Wenglinsky, 2000).

Core Quality: Communication of Content and Skills Knowledge

PROMPT: *Describe how you promote high expectations for student achievement during your instructional time.*

• Effective teachers know that many students view grades as an important measure of success. These teachers encourage students to take risks and strive to meet high expectations by establishing and supporting high expectations themselves; by conveying a "you can do it" attitude; and by providing confidence in the students' abilities while the students are learning what they are capable of doing (Covino & Iwanicki, 1996; Freel, 1998; Peart & Campbell, 1999; Walberg, 1984).

• Effective teachers believe that a self-fulfilling prophecy is at work with regard to student expectations. They act to realize that prophecy by expecting more from students, so that the students' own expectations for success may be raised (Entwisle & Webster, 1973; Mason et al., 1992).

Core Quality: Instructional Complexity

PROMPT: *Pick a topic in your subject area that is often difficult for students to understand. Tell me what the topic is, describe how you explain it to students, and share with me directions for an activity you do to help further students' understanding of that topic.*

• Effective teachers know how content fits into students' lives as well as into the subject matter as a whole, so they present lessons that give facts meaning. They do this by teaching students the content within the larger context of the world, relating material to their day-to-day living and/or other academic subjects (Bloom, 1984).

• Effective teachers also use the context of the lesson to help students relate, organize, and make knowledge a part of their long-term memory (Marzano et al., 1993).

Monitoring Student Progress and Potential

Assessment can be both a continual process and a culminating activity, depending on how it is applied. Teachers informally assess students as they check for understanding through question responses, scan classwork, listen to student questions, and perform a host of other duties. Effective teachers provide both verbal and nonverbal feedback to students on what they are doing well and what can be improved. More formal monitoring of student progress includes written comments on completed assignments, grades, and testing results. Monitoring student progress and potential is a complex assessment process whereby educators use the information they gain to adjust instruction to ensure student growth.

Core Quality: Monitoring Student Progress

PROMPT: *Explain how you share your grading system with students and families.*

• Effective teachers focus on providing feedback that enables students to grow in knowledge and skills. They do this by giving students information about their progress on the intended learning outcomes (Walberg, 1984).

• Effective teachers use verbal and nonverbal feedback in addition to grading assignments in a timely manner (Marzano et al., 2001).

Core Quality: Responding to Student Needs and Abilities

PROMPT: *Tell me how your assessment practices accommodate students' learning needs.*

• Effective teachers sequence activities to promote students' cognitive and developmental growth (Panasuk et al., 2002).

• Effective teachers differentiate instruction and assignments as appropriate for the learner (Stronge et al., 2003; Tomlinson, 1999).

How to Establish a Common Understanding of Interview Response Quality

The TQI protocol uses a scoring rubric to provide a common understanding of the quality of a response. Researchers have found that when question-specific, descriptively anchored rating scales are used, interviewers issue ratings that are more similar than when rubrics are not used (Taylor & Small, 2002). The rubrics contained in both the screening and building-level TQI interview forms were validated as part of a national survey (Hindman, 2004).

The rubrics used in the TQI protocol have four levels to which a response can be assigned: unsatisfactory, developing, proficient, and exemplary. In a larger context, each of these distinctions would indicate the following:

• *Unsatisfactory (i.e., bad).* This applicant does not have what it takes to be an effective teacher. This is an applicant who should not be hired unless the school system is committed to addressing the deficiency.

• *Developing (i.e., OK).* This applicant has the makings of a good teacher but is not there yet. If the school system chooses to extend a contract to this applicant, he or she must receive targeted professional development and support to develop into a proficient teacher.

• *Proficient (i.e., good).* This applicant is most likely a good, solid teacher. Hiring this applicant will be a positive step for the school, students, and other staff members.

• *Exemplary (i.e., excellent).* This applicant is likely a highly effective teacher. This applicant possesses all the characteristics associated with the proficient rating as well as additional skills, abilities, and attributes that would make him or her an outstanding addition to the school system.

The TQI rubrics go one step beyond a standard rating scale by offering descriptions of the specific behaviors associated with each level of performance for each question included in the interview.

Challenges That May Exist When Using the TQI Protocol

The Teacher Quality Index is a highly structured interview protocol. Its strength is a design that aligns the questions to what research has affirmed makes a difference in student learning. For some school systems, challenges of implementing the TQI protocol may include a paradigm shift from making decisions based on "gut reactions" to using a more quantifiable rubric, asking predetermined questions, and considering applicants' reactions.

Shifting the Paradigm

A few people are incredibly attuned to "reading" others and instinctively seem to know how good someone will be in the classroom after just a few minutes of conversation. We all know that first impressions count. It would be naïve to say that how applicants dress or present themselves has no impact on what interviewers think. It is not uncommon to hear people say something like, "I know in the first five minutes if I am going to hire someone." However, the best applicant for the job may not be the same one who makes the best first impression. Consider the fact that it is far easier to buy a professional outfit than it is to develop a repertoire of effective teaching strategies.

One principal shared an example of the problems with first impressions. Two of her teachers were applying for the same position in a neighboring school system that was closer to their homes. The principal would not have minded losing one of the teachers, but the other was an exceptional educator and a lead teacher within the school. Fortunately for this principal, the position went to the less competent teacher. She shared with us, but not with the teacher, that it was probably the interview that decided the matter. The more competent teacher excels with students but has a bad perm, appears frumpy despite trying to look professional, and tends to be nervous in interviews; the less competent teacher—the one selected for the job—has a great wardrobe and a rather polished way of speaking and making things sound good.

"Going with the gut" too often incorporates bias based on first impressions. An applicant who answers one of the first questions really well probably tends to leave interviewers thinking positively even if later questions are not answered as well. This "halo effect" comes about because the interviewers have already made a decision about the applicant and are listening for subsequent responses that reinforce their initial assessment. This also works in the reverse (the "pitchfork effect"). If someone starts off poorly, it is harder to gain ground later in the interview.

The TQI protocol provides a rubric aligned to each question. By asking a question, listening to the response, and rating the quality of that response, interviewers can focus on each answer and assess with a common set of guidelines. Bias diminishes because, no matter what the interviewer thought of the previous response, the current response is assessed on its own merit. The halo and pitchfork effects don't go away completely any more than gut instincts do; however, the protocol helps to contain them and increases the likelihood that the decision will be reached based on all sources of information.

Addressing Concerns about Using Predetermined Questions

Interviewing is just one of many tasks that administrators perform as a part of their jobs. Arguably, it is one of the most important tasks, as it is how new teachers who will have an impact on the school community and student learning are selected. However, despite the importance of interviewing, 69 percent of administrators reported in a national survey that they obtained their interview questions from other administrators (Hindman, 2004). This may suggest that administrators have a great deal of autonomy when it comes to designing their interviews.

The TQI protocol offers human resource and school-based personnel a series of interview questions related to teacher effectiveness. While the questions may be similar to those that administrators already ask, a key difference is how the questions are packaged. The TQI protocol emphasizes not only instruction-related qualities but also other teacher qualities that have been found to reflect teacher effectiveness. Its structured format helps ensure that administrators learn about applicants' teaching practices and abilities related to the various qualities. The predetermined questions focus on getting prospective teachers to talk about what they have done and can do.

Administrators who would prefer to customize their interview protocol by subject area or situation can do so by selecting alternative questions found in the Interviewer's Choice formats, which are included on the CD-ROM provided with this book. Adapting the protocol allows an administrator who is screening novice teachers at a college job fair to ask questions that are not as dependent on classroom experience, addressing instead other related teaching experiences they may have had working with children and youth. Likewise, a building-level interview team can customize the interview protocol to explore topics associated with a particular grade level or subject area.

Addressing Applicants' Reactions

Interviews have a dual purpose that is often overlooked. The primary purpose is for interviewers to make a decision about which applicant to select, but a less frequently considered purpose is for the applicant to get to know the school system. TQI is a highly structured interview protocol that interviewees may not have encountered previously. Applicants in a structured interview may be taken aback by the lack of "casual" dialogue, erroneously inferring that the interviewer does not like them or that they do not want to be a part of such a stiff and formal organization. Additionally, because all the questions are predetermined, there may be situations in which an applicant provides more information in an answer than was really needed and, as a result, has addressed another question. Then, when the interviewer proceeds through the question list, the applicant can be put off by a question asking him or her to provide information already given. The candidate can be left wondering, "Is this interviewer even listening to me?"

The interviewer can address these concerns with little effort. In the first instance, the interviewer should open by explaining that the interview structure is designed to elicit information about the applicant's teaching experience. And in the latter case, interviewer should acknowledge that an interviewee's response to one question has also touched on another question. When that question comes around, the interviewer should offer the applicant an opportunity to address the question further . . . to expand upon what has already been shared.

Ideally, the interview ends with the applicant having an opportunity to ask questions of the interviewer. This will offer the interviewee time to explore other areas of interest about the position, school system, or hiring process. Just as interviewers are seeking someone who will fit and work well in their organization, interviewees are looking for a place where they will enjoy working. The interviewer may be one of the few people in the school system the applicant meets, and the interviewer needs to make a good impression.

Selection Is a Process

If a school or school district is thorough in its review of teacher candidates, it considers a plethora of sources, including: work experience, job-relevant skills and abilities (e.g., computer skills), teacher proficiency examination scores (e.g., PRAXIS), certifications, criminal background checks (required by law in many states), screening interview responses, building level interview interactions, official college transcript, references, writing sample, and sample lesson demonstrations. The TQI interview format can be a vital component in the hiring process. Information exchanged during the dialogue is valuable in assessing an applicant's qualifications for the position, and in determining how well the individual will fit within the organization.

Research related to interviewing and qualities of effective teachers provides the basis for the teacher selection process and the TQI protocol presented here. The process is designed to focus human resource and school personnel on making decisions through an "effectiveness lens." The protocol's design incorporates many of the psychometric properties that have been found to improve the likelihood that the best candidate will be selected. By combining these two areas of research—teacher effectiveness and interview effectiveness—administrators can be in an improved position to select the best teachers from among the available applicants.

5

The Interview Protocol

Having discussed the foundation of the Teacher Quality Index and taken a look at some of its component parts, the time has come to take a look at the full protocol, which is available on the CD-ROM accompanying this book. As noted, the Teacher Quality Index protocol consists of a screening interview and a building-level interview. The CD-ROM contains five forms: both parts of the standard TQI protocol, plus a few variations to provide flexibility. All the forms are easy to download and print out for use in your own setting.

The TQI Screening Interview

The screening interview (see Figure 5.1, beginning on p. 67) has a dual function. Typically, the interview will be used by a member of the district human resources staff to follow up with applicants whose applications scored well on the credential screening; it also can be used for short, job fair interviews. (Remember that if it is used in the latter situation, candidates would still need to submit applications.) The Teacher Quality Index screening interview contains six questions for the applicant and one summary item for the interviewer to consider. Each of the prompts is deliberately general so that human resources professionals can assess responses with a general understanding of pedagogy, the subject area, and student development, given that they may be screening for all levels and subject areas. At the conclusion of the interview, the interviewer totals the subscores that relate to each of the six qualities of effective teachers and indicates if the interviewee should be invited for a building level-interview, in the interviewer's professional judgment. The interview is designed to take approximately 10 to 15 minutes.

The screening interview is included on the CD-ROM in two formats.

Teacher Quality Index Screening Interview—Standard Format (Form 1). This is the same form seen in Figure 5.1. The questions are of a general nature and are useful for most teacher candidates.

Teacher Quality Index Screening Interview—Interviewer's Choice Format (Form 2). This format provides tested and validated alternate prompts for each item. All the options for each item are scored with the same rubric. This provides flexibility and adaptability to the interviewer for each situation and each candidate.

The TQI Building-Level Interview

The TQI building-level interview (see Figure 5.2, beginning on p. 72) is designed to be more in-depth than the screening interview. It encourages applicants to talk about their instructional delivery expertise as well as the planning and assessment functions that are related to the teaching of specific skills and objectives. It contains 13 items distributed across the six qualities of effective teachers. Ideally, the interview would be conducted by a panel of interviewers, at least one of whom is a subject or grade-level expert familiar with the position being filled. In this manner, the interview team would have a person who is knowledgeable about the specific content and skills necessary for student success in the classroom. The building-level interview protocol is designed to take approximately 35 to 45 minutes.

The building-level interview is included on the CD-ROM in three formats.

Teacher Quality Index Building-Level Interview—Standard Format (Form 3). This is the same form seen in Figure 5.2. It is a general form appropriate for all applicants. The wording of the questions is deliberately broad so that an applicant can respond with detailed examples appropriate for the grade level and content area of the position.

Teacher Quality Index Building-Level Interview—Novice Format (Form 4). This format is designed for an interview team meeting with applicants seeking their first teaching position. The questions are tailored to be more appropriate for the novice applicant—teachers with classroom experience of one year or less.

Teacher Quality Index Building-Level Interview—Interviewer's Choice Format (Form 5). This form provides interviewers with the option to ask different questions. It can be used for either novice or veteran teacher candidates. The important thing to remember about this form is that the same questions should be asked of all candidates for a particular position. The interview team would select the questions to be asked prior to interviews from a series of questions associated with each quality area and their accompanying rubrics. As in the Interviewer's Choice format of the screening interview, each question has been tested and validated for use with the same scoring rubric.

Note that the rubric does not change, regardless of the questions asked in the various formats. The reality is that applicants are at different levels in their professional practice. Novice teacher applicants are likely to score in the "Developing" range on the rubric, with a few "Proficient" ratings. These applicants likely are promising teachers and would be good additions to the school, whereas an experienced teacher who scores primarily in the "Developing" range is not a strong candidate for the position. Using the same rubric provides interview teams with a common ground for assessing applicant responses associated with a particular quality area.

FIGURE 5.1
Screening Interview — Standard Format

Applicant's Name _____ Date _____

Teaching Position Sought _____ Time _____

Interview Location ❑ Central Office ❑ Telephone ❑ Job Fair ❑ Other _____

Credential Screen Conducted? ❑ Yes ❑ No
If yes, fill in the information below prior to the interview. If no, ask the applicant to provide this information.

Certification _____ Total Years of Teaching Experience _____

Level of Education _____ Major _____ Minor _____

Graduate Degree(s) _____
Credential screening items will be verified through an application review.

Rating Summary   Interviewer _____

Convert ratings into points and write the number of points in the blank beside the item number(s) listed within each teacher quality area. Unsatisfactory = 0; Developing = 1; Proficient = 2; Exemplary = 3. Then add the points to get an overall score total. The maximum score is 21 points.

Quality Area	Item #	Points	Possible New Hire? ❑ Yes* ❑ No
Prerequisites of Effective Teaching	7		
Teacher as a Person	1		
Classroom Management and Organization	3		
Planning for Instruction	2		
Implementing Instruction	4		
	6		
Monitoring Student Progress and Potential	5		
Overall Score Total			

Directions: This interview contains a total of seven items, including a summary statement, with rubrics for each that are used to rate an applicant's responses.

Immediately after the applicant has responded, score the response by checking the box next to the term that best describes the quality of the applicant's response. At the conclusion of the interview, enter the ratings in the summary box above. Then, based on your professional judgment, determine if the applicant's responses were strong enough to merit his or her consideration for a building-level interview.

*Indicates that the interviewee may be recommended for a building-level interview.

FIGURE 5.1
Screening Interview—Standard Format (*continued*)

1. *Teacher as a Person*
PROMPT: **Share with me why teaching is the profession of choice for you.**

Sample Quality Indicators	Notes
• Displays enthusiasm for learning/subject matter • Interacts with students • Possesses a high level of motivation	

❑ **Unsatisfactory** 0 points	❑ **Developing** 1 point	❑ **Proficient** 2 points	❑ **Exemplary** 3 points
The applicant does not clearly communicate or provide concrete examples.	The applicant clearly communicates a broad idea, but the response lacks specifics.	The applicant communicates with clarity and gives some examples (concrete and abstract).	The applicant effectively communicates with individuals about his or her passion for and dedication to the profession using examples.

2. *Planning for Instruction*
PROMPT: **Think about a lesson you recently taught and describe how you planned for it.**

Sample Quality Indicators	Notes
• Sequences content • Relates concepts to prior knowledge • Selects lesson objectives and aligns activities to them	

❑ **Unsatisfactory** 0 points	❑ **Developing** 1 point	❑ **Proficient** 2 points	❑ **Exemplary** 3 points
The applicant does not make long-range plans to maximize the instructional time during the year.	The applicant does long- and short-range planning, but treats them as isolated planning functions.	The applicant reinforces his or her focus on instruction through allocation of time to address all state and school district objectives by consolidating isolated facts into broader concepts.	The applicant consistently prioritizes instruction by aligning the short-term plans to the long-range plans in order to relate facts and broad concepts to prior and future instruction.

FIGURE 5.1
Screening Interview—Standard Format (*continued*)

3. *Classroom Management and Organization*

PROMPT: **Share with me a time when you had difficulty with a particular student's behavior and what you did to address it.**

Sample Quality Indicators	Notes
• Communicates rules • Monitors behavior and provides feedback • Involves parents/guardians/other school personnel in identifying solutions as appropriate	

❑ **Unsatisfactory** 0 points	❑ **Developing** 1 point	❑ **Proficient** 2 points	☑ **Exemplary** 3 points
The applicant does not communicate clear expectations for behavior to students and the family. Responds primarily with punitive measures.	The applicant inconsistently communicates expectations for behavior and is primarily reactive. Focuses on uniformity and compliance.	The applicant communicates clear expectations about behavior to students and the family and appropriately reinforces those expectations.	The applicant communicates clear expectations for behavior and helps students meet those expectations in a positive and constructive manner.

4. *Implementing Instruction*

PROMPT: **Tell me how you accommodate students' learning needs in the classroom.**

Sample Quality Indicators	Notes
• Holds students individually accountable • Considers students' special needs • Provides differentiated work as appropriate	

❑ **Unsatisfactory** 0 points	❑ **Developing** 1 point	❑ **Proficient** 2 points	❑ **Exemplary** 3 points
The applicant makes no modifications in instructional practices and assessments.	The applicant relies on other sources (e.g., special education teacher, textbook suggestions) to modify activities and assessments.	The applicant differentiates instruction and work for some students (e.g., special education students) as stated in students' plans (e.g., 504, IEP).	The applicant differentiates for specific students, groups, or situations (e.g., gifted, special education).

FIGURE 5.1

FIGURE 5.1
Screening Interview—Standard Format (*continued*)

5. *Monitoring Student Progress and Potential*

PROMPT: **How do you let students in your class know how well they are doing in regard to learning the course and lesson objectives?**

Sample Quality Indicators	Notes
• Provides frequent and timely feedback to students • Offers opportunities for informal and formal assessment • Uses multiple forms of assessment	

❏ **Unsatisfactory** 0 points	❏ **Developing** 1 point	❏ **Proficient** 2 points	❏ **Exemplary** 3 points
The applicant does not use a variety of ongoing and culminating assessments and does not provide ongoing feedback.	The applicant uses a limited variety of ongoing and culminating assessments and provides limited feedback.	The applicant provides a variety of ongoing and culminating assessments to measure student performance and provides feedback on performance.	The applicant creates, selects, and effectively uses a variety of ongoing and culminating assessments to determine grades and regularly interprets and communicates student progress.

6. *Implementing Instruction*

PROMPT: **Describe how you promote high expectations for student achievement during your instructional time.**

Sample Quality Indicators	Notes
• Sets high expectations for self • Provides strategies for students to achieve • Emphasizes student responsibility	

❏ **Unsatisfactory** 0 points	❏ **Developing** 1 point	❏ **Proficient** 2 points	❏ **Exemplary** 3 points
The applicant places the responsibility for student achievement on the students.	The applicant encourages students to participate in their own learning while assuming primary responsibility for the students' learning.	The applicant promotes enthusiasm for learning and encourages students to be active participants in their learning.	The applicant communicates a high regard for students and high expectations, offering examples of how this looks in practice to meet the varying levels of students' needs.

FIGURE 5.1
Screening Interview—Standard Format (*continued*)

7. *Prerequisites of Effective Teaching*

THIS IS NOT A PROMPT. Based on the applicant's interview, provide an overall rating of the impression made by the applicant in terms of how well the applicant spoke and conveyed his or her knowledge of the content, pedagogy, and students.

Sample Quality Indicators		Notes	
• Uses current and accurate knowledge • Uses standard English grammar • Is knowledgeable about students			
❑ **Unsatisfactory** 0 points	❑ **Developing** 1 point	❑ **Proficient** 2 points	❑ **Exemplary** 3 points
The applicant makes substantive errors or displays a lack of the knowledge critical to the functioning of a teacher.	The applicant displays an adequate amount of knowledge, but needs to develop professionally	The applicant displays satisfactory knowledge expected of the content, pedagogy, and students.	The applicant displays a deep understanding of the content, pedagogy, and students.

Conclude the interview by doing the following:

- Ask if the applicant has any questions.

- Let the applicant know when he or she is likely to hear from the school district again.

- Thank the applicant for his or her time.

FIGURE 5.2
Building-Level Interview—Standard Format

Applicant's Name _____ Date _____

Teaching Position Sought _____ Time _____

Rating Summary   Interviewer _____

Convert ratings into points and write the number of points in the blank beside the item numbers listed within each teacher quality area. Unsatisfactory = 0; Developing = 1; Proficient = 2; Exemplary = 3. Then add the points to get an overall score total. The maximum score is 39 points.

Quality Area	Item #	Points	Positives and Negatives (+/−)
Prerequisites of Effective Teaching	13		*Based on the interview, list the applicant's positive and negative qualities with respect to this position.*
Teacher as a Person	1		
	8		
	11		
Classroom Management and Organization	2		
	5		
Planning for Instruction	3		
	6		
Implementing Instruction	4		
	9		
	10		
Monitoring Student Progress and Potential	7		
	12		
Overall Score Total			**Applicant's Rank: _____ out of _____**

Directions: This interview contains a total of 13 items, including a summary statement, with rubrics for each that are used to rate an applicant's responses.

Immediately after the applicant has responded, score the response by checking the box next to the term that best describes the quality of the applicant's response. At the conclusion of the interview, enter the ratings in the summary box above and list the applicant's positive and negative qualities with respect to this position.

When all the interviews have been concluded, rank the interviewees based on all the available information, such as resume, application, and interview. The total score and rank are for discussion of the applicants, not indicators of a final selection decision.

FIGURE 5.2
Building-Level Interview—Standard Format (*continued*)

1. *Teacher as a Person*
PROMPT: **Share with me why teaching is the profession of choice for you.**

Sample Quality Indicators		Notes	
<ul><li>Displays enthusiasm for learning/subject matter</li><li>Interacts with students</li><li>Possesses a high level of motivation</li></ul>			
❏ **Unsatisfactory** 0 points	❏ **Developing** 1 point	❏ **Proficient** 2 points	❏ **Exemplary** 3 points
The applicant does not clearly communicate or provide concrete examples.	The applicant clearly communicates a broad idea, but the response lacks specifics.	The applicant communicates with clarity and gives some examples (concrete and abstract).	The applicant effectively communicates with individuals about his or her passion for and dedication to the profession using examples.

2. *Classroom Management and Organization*
PROMPT: **Tell me what you do with students during the first few weeks of the school year to establish a positive classroom environment.**

Sample Quality Indicators		Notes	
<ul><li>Establishes clear rules and routines</li><li>Gets to know the students</li><li>Offers opportunities for students to be successful with the classroom guidelines</li></ul>			
❏ **Unsatisfactory** 0 points	❏ **Developing** 1 point	❏ **Proficient** 2 points	❏ **Exemplary** 3 points
The applicant presents the rules and starts instruction during the first week of school but does not give examples of how he or she builds rapport with students or reinforces the classroom guidelines.	The applicant shares classroom operating procedures with students and families but offers limited opportunities for students to practice the routines and be successful at following the rules after the initial introduction.	The applicant spends more time in the beginning weeks of school establishing routines and reinforcing the rules so that students know what is expected of them. These expectations, as appropriate, are communicated to students' families.	The applicant builds a classroom community by providing opportunities for students to take responsibility and have ownership of the classroom.

FIGURE 5.2
Building-Level Interview—Standard Format (*continued*)

3. *Planning for Instruction*
PROMPT: **Share with me your long- and short-term planning process for instruction.**

Sample Quality Indicators	Notes
• Sequences content • Relates concepts to prior knowledge • Selects lesson objectives and aligns activities to them	

❏ **Unsatisfactory** 0 points	❏ **Developing** 1 point	❏ **Proficient** 2 points	❏ **Exemplary** 3 points
The applicant does not make long-range plans to maximize the instructional time during the year.	The applicant does long- and short-range planning but treats them as isolated planning functions.	The applicant reinforces his or her focus on instruction through allocation of time to address all state and school district objectives by consolidating isolated facts into broader concepts.	The applicant consistently prioritizes instruction by aligning the short-term plans to the long-range plans in order to enrich and expand the state standards and district curriculum.

4. *Implementing Instruction*
PROMPT: **Describe how you engage students in their learning.**

Sample Quality Indicators	Notes
• Solicits students' comments and questions • Uses a variety of hands-on/minds-on activities • Monitors students' understanding and adjusts lesson pacing or activities	

❏ **Unsatisfactory** 0 points	❏ **Developing** 1 point	❏ **Proficient** 2 points	❏ **Exemplary** 3 points
The applicant makes few or no changes in activities to meet the needs of students or to enhance engagement.	The applicant makes minor changes in activities to meet the changing needs and interests of students and to enhance engagement.	The applicant modifies activities to address the changing needs of students and to enhance their active engagement.	The applicant systematically designs activities for different students and achieves high levels of active engagement.

FIGURE 5.2
Building-Level Interview—Standard Format (*continued*)

5. *Classroom Management and Organization*
PROMPT: **Tell me about a frustrating situation involving a student's actions and how you resolved it when you approached the student's parents/guardians about the behavior.**

Sample Quality Indicators		Notes	
• Communicates rules • Demonstrates respect for students and the family • Monitors behavior and provides feedback • Involves parents/guardians and other school personnel in identifying solutions as appropriate			
☐ **Unsatisfactory** 0 points	☐ **Developing** 1 point	☐ **Proficient** 2 points	☑ **Exemplary** 3 points
The applicant does not communicate clear expectations for behavior to students and the family. Responds primarily with punitive measures; contacting the parents/guardians is a matter of procedure or carrying through on a consequence.	The applicant inconsistently communicates expectations for behavior and is primarily reactive. Focuses on uniformity and compliance. Seeks support from home for his or her concerns and the need for the student's behavior to improve.	The applicant communicates clear expectations about behavior to students and the parent/guardian. Sensitively inquires if there is anything the teacher should know that might help the situation. Shares with the family the teacher's plan of action.	The applicant communicates clear expectations for behavior and helps students meet those expectations in a positive and constructive manner. Seeks to create win-win situations by involving appropriate people in supporting the student in making more positive behavioral choices.

6. *Planning for Instruction*
PROMPT: **Think about a unit you have taught. Tell me why you selected particular instructional strategies to teach the curriculum.**

Sample Quality Indicators		Notes	
• Uses a range of strategies • Identifies the available resources • Selects problem-solving, hands-on, and interactive strategies and resources			
☐ **Unsatisfactory** 0 points	☐ **Developing** 1 point	☐ **Proficient** 2 points	☐ **Exemplary** 3 points
The applicant does not vary his or her narrow set of instructional strategies.	The applicant uses a limited number of instructional strategies with limited attempts to appeal to student needs or interests.	The applicant uses a variety of instructional strategies that appeal to the interests of different students.	The applicant uses a wide range of instructional strategies diagnostically to enhance student understanding of concepts.

FIGURE 5.2
Building-Level Interview—Standard Format (*continued*)

7. *Monitoring Student Progress and Potential*
PROMPT: **Tell me how your assessment practices accommodate students' learning needs.**

Sample Quality Indicators		Notes	
• Holds students individually accountable • Considers students' special needs • Provides differentiated assessments			
❑ **Unsatisfactory** 0 points	❑ **Developing** 1 point	❑ **Proficient** 2 points	❑ **Exemplary** 3 points
The applicant makes no modifications in instructional practices and assessments.	The applicant relies on other sources (e.g., special education teacher, textbook suggestions) to modify activities and assessments.	The applicant differentiates assessment for some students (e.g., special education students) as stated in students' plans (e.g., 504, IEP).	The applicant uses assessments that are differentiated for specific students, groups, or situations (e.g., gifted, special education).

8. *Teacher as a Person*
PROMPT: **Give me an example of how you establish and maintain a rapport with your students.**

Sample Quality Indicators		Notes	
• Knows students' interests • Uses humor • Interacts in more informal settings (e.g., in the lunchroom, at school events such as band concerts)			
❑ **Unsatisfactory** 0 points	❑ **Developing** 1 point	❑ **Proficient** 2 points	❑ **Exemplary** 3 points
The applicant shares examples that are uncaring or distant with regard to student interactions.	The applicant focuses on establishing a teacher-student rapport with clear boundaries.	The applicant is caring with his or her students and provides in-school examples (e.g., classroom, lunchroom, ball games) demonstrating that he or she is interested in the students as individuals.	The applicant provides clear examples of interactions with students in the school (e.g., classroom, band concerts) and outside of the school (e.g., community events) that are caring and authentic.

FIGURE 5.2
Building-Level Interview—Standard Format (*continued*)

9. *Implementing Instruction*
PROMPT: **How do you use technology during your instruction?** *(Note: If needed, suggest types of technology, such as computers, graphing calculators, overheads, laserdiscs, and DVDs.)*

Sample Quality Indicators		Notes	
• Creates tasks to increase students' proficiency with technology • Considers technology as a broad term not limited to computers • Integrates technology into meaningful lessons			
❑ **Unsatisfactory** 0 points	❑ **Developing** 1 point	❑ **Proficient** 2 points	❑ **Exemplary** 3 points
The applicant indicates a lack of knowledge or competence in using technology.	The applicant has limited integration of technology and authentic student work.	The applicant uses the available technology as appropriate to instructional objectives to increase students' proficiency with the technology or technology application.	The applicant offers examples of how technology is integrated into lessons in order to increase students' understanding of the content as well as encourage their decision making about how to use technology appropriately.

10. *Implementing Instruction*
PROMPT: **Pick a topic in your subject area that is often difficult for students to understand. Tell me what the topic is and how you explain it to students, and share with me directions for an activity you do to help further students' understanding of that topic.**

Sample Quality Indicators		Notes	
• Provides a clear example with step-by-step directions • Uses multiple learning modalities • Selects an example appropriate to the content area			
❑ **Unsatisfactory** 0 points	❑ **Developing** 1 point	❑ **Proficient** 2 points	❑ **Exemplary** 3 points
The applicant gives a confusing example and/or directions.	The applicant provides an inadequate answer; however, it does demonstrate some knowledge.	The applicant gives a clear example with opportunities for guided practice as well as targeted instruction for students needing more support.	The applicant clearly articulates the problem area with the topic and provides a clear example that is followed by a plan for how to meet the individual needs of students who require more assistance.

FIGURE 5.2

Building-Level Interview—Standard Format (*continued*)

11. *Teacher as a Person*

PROMPT: **Think about a lesson that did not meet your expectations, despite planning and preparation. Tell me what you considered when planning to readdress the topic with your students and describe how you altered your approach.**

Sample Quality Indicators	Notes
• Identifies strengths and weaknesses • Targets efforts for change/revision • Demonstrates a high sense of efficacy	

❑ **Unsatisfactory** 0 points	❑ **Developing** 1 point	❑ **Proficient** 2 points	❑ **Exemplary** 3 points
The applicant focuses on management-related issues without consideration of instructionally-related issues.	The applicant addresses instructional and curricular issues in a limited fashion with minimal reflection.	The applicant reflects on his or her work both formally and informally in order to improve his or her teaching and the students' learning.	The applicant consistently reflects on his or her work, seeks outside counsel from appropriate sources, and strives to identify ways to improve the learning experience for students.

12. *Monitoring Student Progress and Potential*

PROMPT: **Tell me what you do when a large number of students perform poorly on a formal assessment.**

Sample Quality Indicators	Notes
• Identifies teacher as responsible for student learning • Identifies instruction and assessment as possible sources for failure • Identifies corrective measures	

❑ **Unsatisfactory** 0 points	❑ **Developing** 1 point	❑ **Proficient** 2 points	❑ **Exemplary** 3 points
The applicant places responsibility for student achievement on students and takes little to no personal responsibility.	The applicant recognizes that a problem exists but does not reteach or reassess.	The applicant identifies self as integral component in teaching and learning. Identifies some strategies for addressing poor performance.	The applicant clearly identifies possible sources for poor student performance and appropriately implements corrective measures.

FIGURE 5.2
Building-Level Interview—Standard Format (*continued*)

13. *Prerequisites of Effective Teaching*
THIS IS NOT A PROMPT. Based on the applicant's interview, provide an overall rating of the applicant's knowledge of the content matter.

Sample Quality Indicators		*Notes*	
• Uses current and accurate knowledge • Integrates appropriate skills • Uses appropriate instructional strategies			
❏ **Unsatisfactory** 0 points	❏ **Developing** 1 point	❏ **Proficient** 2 points	❏ **Exemplary** 3 points
The applicant makes substantive errors or displays a lack of knowledge critical to the functioning of a teacher.	The applicant displays an adequate amount of knowledge, but needs to develop professionally.	The applicant displays satisfactory knowledge of content, pedagogy, and students.	The applicant displays a deep understanding of content, pedagogy, and students.

Conclude the interview by doing the following:

• Ask if the applicant has any questions.

• Let the applicant know when he or she is likely to hear from the school district again.

• Thank the applicant for his or her time.

Rating Interview Responses

Imagine that you are conducting an interview and have just given the applicant the first prompt in the TQI interview: "Share with me why teaching is the profession of choice for you." And now imagine the applicant saying something like, "Oh, I've always wanted to be a teacher. I just love little children." Your task now is to rate that response. Would you rate it as "Unsatisfactory," "Developing," "Proficient," or "Exemplary"?

Let's consider the applicant's response using Figure 6.1, which shows the complete item as it appears on the interview form. Note the sample quality indicators: items found in the research literature associated with the particular quality of effective teachers being queried. The response of our imaginary applicant did not hit on any of the sample indicators. This is not detrimental in and of itself because the sample quality indicators are merely items you might hear in a well-articulated response. They are examples only.

Suppose your initial thought is that this applicant's response is "Unsatisfactory." Yet on a positive note, imagine that the applicant's face lit up the room as she spoke, making the response sound strong even though the message was weak. You might make a note of this observation in the space provided to the right of the indicators.

The advantage of using a common rubric is that interviewers have a leveling ground for their assessments of responses. Take another look at the four-part, behaviorally-anchored rubric in Figure 6.1. Now go ahead and

FIGURE 6.1
Sample TQI Interview Question

1. *Teacher as a Person*
PROMPT: **Share with me why teaching is the profession of choice for you.**

Sample Quality Indicators	Notes		
• Displays enthusiasm for learning/subject matter • Interacts with students • Possesses a high level of motivation			
❑ **Unsatisfactory** 0 points	❑ **Developing** 1 point	❑ **Proficient** 2 points	❑ **Exemplary** 3 points
The applicant does not clearly communicate or provide concrete examples.	The applicant clearly communicates a broad idea, but the response lacks specifics.	The applicant communicates with clarity and gives some examples (concrete and abstract).	The applicant effectively communicates with individuals about his or her passion for and dedication to the profession using examples.

make a final decision about the quality of this imagined applicant's response to the prompt.

One perception might be that this applicant's response could be considered "Developing," as the applicant clearly stated a love of students and a desire to teach. However, the rubric shows that a lack of concrete examples and elaboration is a component of an "Unsatisfactory" response. The applicant did not clearly communicate or provide concrete examples. Your first instinct was right on target, and it was confirmed by the research-based rubric. So far, so good.

Practice Activity

As you know, during an actual interview there is little time to read rubrics and rate responses because the exchange of questions and answers has its own cadence. Being familiar with the rubrics associated with each question can help interviewers to make an initial assessment of the response before the next question is asked. And the way to familiarize yourself with the TQI interview protocol is to practice aligning your perceptions with the protocol's research-based rubric.

Figure 6.2 provides a practice activity similar to the example just given. It contains one-line summaries designed to capture the spirit and message of how an applicant may respond to a given question. For each question, there are three different responses to rate. At first, you may feel uncomfortable applying a rating to a one-liner, but try it. The one-line summaries were field-tested with public school administrators throughout the United States, who did a longer version of the activity. Their responses support the research-based target ratings presented in the answers section following the activity.

An advantage of using the TQI protocol is that it increases *intrarater reliability:* how consistent an interviewer is when applying ratings to the applicant's responses. As discussed, during an interview, many factors influence the ratings an interviewer gives. For instance, an applicant may give a strong answer to one question but a weak answer to the next. In such a case, the interviewer may be inclined to give the applicant the benefit of the doubt and discount the weak response. When a rubric is associated with each question, the interviewer can score items and notice trends in the applicant's responses related to particular areas associated with effective teachers.

The practice activity provides a good introduction to the TQI protocol. Members of an interview team can complete the activity independently and then join together to discuss it to increase *interrater reliability:* the degree to which different interviewers respond to the same applicant in the same manner. Most administrators involved in group hiring decisions have experienced situations where someone who tends to see the world through rose-colored glasses gives all applicants high ratings, while another group member consistently gives low ratings. The rubric is a way of getting everyone on the team to use the same criteria to assess a response.

Note that the practice activity can also be used as a role-playing activity for your interview team. Take turns being the starry-eyed applicant, or the grumpy interviewee, or the too controlling teacher.

FIGURE 6.2
Practice Activity for Interview Teams or Individuals

Directions: This activity is designed to help associate statements describing teacher applicants' responses with administrators' judgment of the strength of the statements. Under each boldfaced question are three statements summarizing the responses different teacher applicants may offer to the prompt. Consider what level of proficiency a teacher applicant who makes such a statement would be likely to represent. Place a check mark in the box to the right of the statement to match the statement to the level of proficiency. The statements for each question may not represent all levels.

There are four levels for your consideration:

U—Unsatisfactory. *The applicant does not have what it takes to be an effective teacher.*
D—Developing. *The applicant has the makings of a good teacher but is not there yet.*
P—Proficient. *The applicant is most likely a good, solid teacher.*
E—Exemplary. *The applicant is likely a highly effective teacher.*

Items 1–3 focus on gathering information about the applicant relating to the quality area *Teacher as a Person.*

1. Share with me why teaching is the profession of choice for you.

	U	D	P	E
a. Communicates an idealistic but ungrounded view of teaching	☐	☐	☐	☐
b. Communicates a passion for seeing students enjoying learning	☐	☐	☐	☐
c. Communicates a broad idea that lacks specificity	☐	☐	☐	☐

Unsatisfactory	Developing	Proficient	Exemplary
The applicant does not clearly communicate or provide concrete examples.	The applicant clearly communicates a broad idea, but the response lacks specifics.	The applicant communicates with clarity and gives some examples (concrete and abstract).	The applicant effectively communicates with individuals about his or her passion for and dedication to the profession using examples.

2. Give me an example of how you establish and maintain a rapport with your students.

	U	D	P	E
a. Says it is hard to relate to students who are so different from the teacher or other students he or she has taught	☐	☐	☐	☐
b. Focuses on the teacher's role in controlling students	☐	☐	☐	☐
c. Interacts and knows students by group interests	☐	☐	☐	☐

Unsatisfactory	Developing	Proficient	Exemplary
The applicant shares examples that are uncaring or distant with regard to student interactions.	The applicant focuses on establishing a teacher-student rapport with clear boundaries.	The applicant is caring with his or her students and provides in-school examples (e.g., classroom, lunchroom, ball games) demonstrating that he or she is interested in students as individuals.	The applicant provides clear examples of interactions with students in the school (e.g., classroom, band concerts) and outside of the school (e.g., community events) that are caring and authentic.

FIGURE 6.2
Practice Activity for Interview Teams or Individuals *(continued)*

3. Think about a lesson that did not meet your expectations, despite planning and preparation. Tell me what you considered when planning to readdress the topic with your students and describe how you altered your approach.

	U	D	P	E
a. Focuses on non-teacher-related issues	☐	☐	☐	☐
b. Addresses the issue with limited evidence of reflection	☐	☐	☐	☐
c. Shows evidence of using reflection to improve teaching	☐	☐	☐	☐

Unsatisfactory	Developing	Proficient	Exemplary
The applicant focuses on management-related issues without consideration of instructionally related issues.	The applicant addresses instructional and curricular issues in a limited fashion with minimal reflection.	The applicant reflects on his or her work both formally and informally in order to improve his or her teaching and the students' learning.	The applicant consistently reflects on his or her work, seeks outside counsel from peers, and strives to identify ways to improve the learning experience for students.

Items 4–5 focus on gathering information about the applicant relating to the quality area *Classroom Management and Organization.*

4. Tell me what you do with students during the first few weeks of the school year to establish a positive classroom environment.

	U	D	P	E
a. Builds a classroom community through student ownership	☐	☐	☐	☐
b. Spends time at the start of the school year reinforcing routines so students can work independently	☐	☐	☐	☐
c. Responds to students who are off task and redirects them	☐	☐	☐	☐

Unsatisfactory	Developing	Proficient	Exemplary
The applicant presents the rules and starts instruction during the first week of school, but does not build a rapport with students or reinforce the classroom guidelines.	The applicant shares classroom operating procedures with students and families but offers limited opportunities for students to practice the routines and be successful at following the rules after the initial introduction.	The applicant spends more time in the beginning weeks of school establishing routines and reinforcing the rules so that students know what is expected of them. These expectations are communicated to students' families.	The applicant builds a classroom community by providing opportunities for students to take responsibility and have ownership of the classroom.

FIGURE 6.2
Practice Activity for Interview Teams or Individuals *(continued)*

5. Share with me a time you had difficulty with a particular student's behavior and what you did to address it.

	U	D	P	E
a. Disciplines students using punitive measures	☐	☐	☐	☐
b. Focuses on the need for strict discipline measures	☐	☐	☐	☐
c. Reinforces the behavioral expectations	☐	☐	☐	☐

Unsatisfactory	Developing	Proficient	Exemplary
The applicant does not communicate clear expectations for behavior to students and parents. Responds primarily with punitive measures.	The applicant inconsistently communicates expectations for behavior and is primarily reactive. Focuses on uniformity and compliance.	The applicant communicates clear expectations about behavior to students and parents and appropriately reinforces those expectations.	The applicant communicates clear expectations for behavior and helps students meet those expectations in a positive and constructive manner.

Items 6–7 focus on gathering information about the applicant relating to the quality area *Planning for Instruction.*

6. Share with me your long- and short-term planning process for instruction.

	U	D	P	E
a. Treats long- and short-term planning as isolated planning functions	☐	☐	☐	☐
b. Uses both long- and short-term planning, relying heavily on short-term planning	☐	☐	☐	☐
c. Indicates that long-range planning is not useful as there are too many interruptions in the school year	☐	☐	☐	☐

Unsatisfactory	Developing	Proficient	Exemplary
The applicant does not make long-range plans to maximize the instructional time during the year.	The applicant does long- and short-range planning but treats them as isolated planning functions.	The applicant reinforces his or her focus on instruction through allocation of time to address all state and school district objectives by consolidating isolated facts into broader concepts.	The applicant consistently prioritizes instruction by aligning the short-term plans to the long-range plans in order to enrich and expand the state standards and district curriculum.

FIGURE 6.2

Practice Activity for Interview Teams or Individuals *(continued)*

7. Think about a unit you have taught. Tell me why you selected particular instructional strategies to teach the curriculum.

	U	D	P	E
a. Diagnostically uses a wide range of instructional strategies to optimize student learning	☐	☐	☐	☐
b. Refers to a few instructional strategies he or she knows well	☐	☐	☐	☐
c. Selects strategies that appeal to students' learning styles	☐	☐	☐	☐

Unsatisfactory	Developing	Proficient	Exemplary
The teacher does not vary his or her narrow set of instructional strategies.	The teacher uses a limited number of instructional strategies with limited attempts to appeal to student needs or interests.	The teacher uses a variety of instructional strategies that appeal to the interests of different students.	The teacher diagnostically uses a wide range of instructional strategies to enhance student understanding of concepts.

Items 8–11 focus on gathering information about the applicant relating to the quality area *Implementing Instruction.*

8. Describe how you engage students in their learning.

	U	D	P	E
a. Systematically designs differentiated learning activities	☐	☐	☐	☐
b. Has a "one size fits all" approach to instruction	☐	☐	☐	☐
c. Provides some activities designed to capitalize on student interest	☐	☐	☐	☐

Unsatisfactory	Developing	Proficient	Exemplary
The teacher makes few or no changes in activities to meet the needs of students or to enhance engagement.	The teacher makes minor changes in activities to meet the changing needs and interests of students and to enhance engagement.	The teacher modifies activities to address the changing needs of students and to enhance their active engagement.	The teacher systematically designs activities for different students and achieves high levels of active engagement.

9. Describe how you promote high expectations for student achievement during your instructional time.

	U	D	P	E
a. Offers examples of what meeting varying levels of expectation looks like on particular assignments	☐	☐	☐	☐
b. Encourages students to participate in their learning	☐	☐	☐	☐
c. Suggests that student achievement is the job of the student and is influenced slightly by the teacher	☐	☐	☐	☐

Unsatisfactory	Developing	Proficient	Exemplary
The applicant places the responsibility for student achievement on the students.	The applicant encourages students to participate in their own learning while assuming primary responsibility for the students' learning.	The applicant promotes enthusiasm for learning and encourages students to be active participants in their learning.	The applicant communicates a high regard for students and high expectations offering examples of how this looks in practice to meet the varying levels of students' needs.

FIGURE 6.2
Practice Activity for Interview Teams or Individuals *(continued)*

10. How do you use technology during your instruction?

		U	D	P	E
a.	Is uncomfortable with technology	☐	☐	☐	☐
b.	Uses available technology as appropriate to instructional objectives	☐	☐	☐	☐
c.	Offers examples of how technology and other related resources are integrated into meaningful lessons	☐	☐	☐	☐

Unsatisfactory	Developing	Proficient	Exemplary
The applicant indicates a lack of knowledge or competence in using technology.	The applicant has limited integration of technology and authentic student work.	The applicant uses the available technology as appropriate to instructional objectives to increase students' proficiency with the technology or technology application.	The applicant offers examples of how technology is integrated into lessons in order to increase students' understanding of the content as well as encourage their decision making about how to use technology appropriately.

11. Pick a topic in your subject area that is often difficult for students to understand. Tell me what the topic is and how you explain it to students, and share with me directions for an activity you do to further students' understanding of that topic.

		U	D	P	E
a.	Offers plenty of instructional examples and guided practice	☐	☐	☐	☐
b.	Gives confusing examples and directions in the example selected	☐	☐	☐	☐
c.	Uses clear examples and step-by-step directions	☐	☐	☐	☐

Unsatisfactory	Developing	Proficient	Exemplary
The applicant gives a confusing example and/or directions.	The applicant provides an inadequate answer; however, it does demonstrate some knowledge.	The applicant gives a clear example with opportunities for guided practice as well as targeted instruction for students needing more support.	The applicant clearly articulates the problem area with the topic and provides a clear example that is followed by a plan of how to meet individual needs of students who require more assistance.

FIGURE 6.2
Practice Activity for Interview Teams or Individuals *(continued)*

Items 12–13 focus on gathering information about the applicant relating to the quality area *Monitoring Student Progress and Potential.*

		U	D	P	E
12.	**Explain how you share your grading system with students and families.**				
a.	Provides adequate feedback on performance	□	□	□	□
b.	Prefers to base grades solely on culminating assignments (e.g., tests).	□	□	□	□
c.	Interprets and communicates student progress through regularly timed reports that are issued in addition to the school's marking period	□	□	□	□

Unsatisfactory	Developing	Proficient	Exemplary
The applicant does not use a variety of ongoing and culminating assessments and does not provide ongoing feedback.	The applicant uses a limited variety of ongoing and culminating assessments and provides limited feedback.	The applicant provides a variety of ongoing and culminating assessments to measure student performance and provides feedback on performance.	The applicant creates, selects, and effectively uses a variety of ongoing and culminating assessments to determine grades and regularly interprets and communicates student progress.

		U	D	P	E
13.	**Tell me how your assessment practices accommodate students' learning needs.**				
a.	Gives modified assessments when they are prepared by the special education teacher	□	□	□	□
b.	Differentiates as appropriate for students of all ability levels.	□	□	□	□
c.	Accommodates only when there is an IEP or 504 plan being enforced	□	□	□	□

Unsatisfactory	Developing	Proficient	Exemplary
The applicant makes no modifications in instructional practices and assessments.	The applicant relies on other sources (e.g., special education teacher, textbook suggestions) to modify activities and assessments.	The applicant differentiates assessment for special education students as stated in students' plans (e.g., 504, IEP).	The applicant uses assessments that are differentiated for specific students, groups, or situations (e.g., gifted, special education).

Answers

Check your scoring against Figure 6.3 and analyze the results. For each response, a rating within one rating level of the research base's response is considered acceptable (Stronge et al., 2002). However, being within one rating level is more likely to occur when listening to full responses than with the one-line summaries, as applicants' actual responses may seem to straddle two ratings. In practice, your professional judgment comes heavily into play in such a situation. There is always room for personal interpretation; however, by using a common rubric, the ratings should be more standardized (i.e., interrater reliability will be stronger). The goal of the practice activity is to enhance your use of the rubrics so that your rating of applicants' responses is based on the applicable teacher effectiveness research.

FIGURE 6.3
Research-Based* Answers to the Practice Activity

---

1. **Share with me why teaching is the profession of choice for you.**
   a. Communicates an idealistic but ungrounded view of teaching. . . . . DEVELOPING
   b. Communicates a passion for seeing students enjoying learning. . . . . EXEMPLARY
   c. Communicates a broad idea that lacks specificity. . . . . DEVELOPING

2. **Give me an example of how you establish and maintain a rapport with your students.**
   a. Says it is hard to relate to students who are so different from the teacher or other students he
      or she has taught. . . . . UNSATISFACTORY
   b. Focuses on the teacher's role in controlling students. . . . . UNSATISFACTORY
   c. Interacts and knows students by group interests . . . . PROFICIENT

3. **Think about a lesson that did not meet your expectations, despite planning and preparation. Tell me what you considered when planning to readdress the topic with your students and describe how you altered your approach.**
   a. Focuses on non-teacher-related issues. . . . . UNSATISFACTORY
   b. Addresses the issue with limited evidence of reflection. . . . . DEVELOPING
   c. Shows evidence of using reflection to improve teaching . . . . PROFICIENT

*The research base consists of qualities of effective teachers research for the item statement and the results from a national study (Hindman, 2004) for the rating.

(continues)

FIGURE 6.3

Research-Based Answers to the Practice Activity (*continued*)

---

4. Tell me what you do with students during the first few weeks of the school year to establish a positive classroom environment.
a. Builds a classroom community through student ownership . . . . EXEMPLARY
b. Spends time at the start of the school year reinforcing routines so students can work independently . . . . PROFICIENT
c. Responds to students who are off task and redirects them . . . . PROFICIENT

5. Share with me a time you had difficulty with a particular student's behavior and what you did to address it.
a. Disciplines students using punitive measures . . . . UNSATISFACTORY
b. Focuses on the need for strict discipline measures. . . . . DEVELOPING
c. Reinforces behavioral expectations . . . . PROFICIENT

6. Share with me your long- and short-term planning process for instruction.
a. Treats long- and short-term planning as isolated planning functions . . . . DEVELOPING
b. Uses both long- and short-term planning, relying heavily on short-term . . . . PROFICIENT
c. Indicates that long-range planning is not useful as there are too many interruptions in the school year . . . . . . UNSATISFACTORY

7. Think about a unit you have taught. Tell me why you selected particular instructional strategies to teach the curriculum.
a. Diagnostically uses a wide range of instructional strategies to optimize student learning . . . . EXEMPLARY
b. Refers to a few instructional strategies he or she knows well. . . . . DEVELOPING
c. Selects strategies that appeal to students' learning styles . . . . PROFICIENT

8. Describe how you engage students in their learning.
a. Systematically designs differentiated learning activities . . . . EXEMPLARY
b. Has a "one size fits all" approach to instruction . . . . UNSATISFACTORY
c. Provides some activities designed to capitalize on student interest . . . . DEVELOPING

9. Describe how you promote high expectations for student achievement during your instructional time.
a. Offers examples of what meeting varying levels of expectation looks like on particular assignments . . . . EXEMPLARY
b. Encourages students to participate in their learning . . . . DEVELOPING
c. Suggests that student achievement is the job of the student and is influenced slightly by the teacher . . . . . UNSATISFACTORY

10. How do you use technology as part of your instruction?
a. Is uncomfortable with technology . . . . UNSATISFACTORY
b. Uses available technology as appropriate to instructional objectives. . . . . PROFICIENT
c. Offers examples of how technology and other related resources are integrated into meaningful lessons . . . . EXEMPLARY

FIGURE 6.3
FIGURE 6.3
Research-Based Answers to the Practice Activity (*continued*)

11. **Pick a topic in your subject area that is often difficult for students to understand. Tell me what the topic is and how you explain it to students, and share with me directions for an activity you do to further students' understanding of that topic.**
   a. Offers plenty of instructional examples and guided practice . . . . EXEMPLARY
   b. Gives confusing examples and directions in the example selected . . . . UNSATISFACTORY
   c. Uses clear examples and step-by-step directions. . . . . PROFICIENT

12. **Explain how you share your grading system with students and families.**
   a. Provides adequate feedback on performance . . . . PROFICIENT
   b. Prefers to base grades solely on culminating assignments (e.g., tests) . . . . UNSATISFACTORY
   c. Interprets and communicates student progress through regularly timed reports that are issued in addition to the school's marking period . . . . EXEMPLARY

13. **Tell me how your assessment practices accommodate students' learning needs.**
   a. Gives modified assessments when they are prepared by the special education teacher . . . . DEVELOPING
   b. Differentiates as appropriate for students of all ability levels . . . . EXEMPLARY
   c. Accommodates only when there is an IEP or 504 plan being enforced . . . . UNSATISFACTORY

Questions You May Have

The practice activity is just that—*practice*. In working with the TQI protocol for the first time, you may have formed some questions. Here are answers to common queries.

How can I give a rating to just a one-line summary?

Sometimes less can be more. Being given just a few words allows you to focus on the idea that is communicated without the added dynamic of word usage, engaging language, and grammar while you apply the rubric to the summary. You may find it helpful to recall an applicant whose response you would characterize the same way and then fit that response to the rubric.

I can't hit the target. What can I do?

The rubrics are a tool to increase interrater reliability. In your analysis of your responses, you may have noticed that you were high or low. You may have skimmed the rubrics and rated the summary according to your own professional experience. The reality is that some schools and school systems attract stronger applicants, so what may be a proficient response in most of the country is a developing response in your mind. The reverse may also be true. The TQI interview is not about changing your high expectations for the teachers you select; it is about standardizing how you rate applicants so that the same criteria are being used to assess teachers regardless of who is interviewing them. Go back and look at the target response and then read the rubric description associated with that target. Reflect on how that particular one-line summary fits within the description.

I seem to find myself debating between two ratings. What should I do?

The TQI protocol is one part of a hiring process that likely began when the applicant submitted an application. The rubric gives you a way to evaluate all responses with the same criteria. If you are on the fence between two ratings, mark your intuitive response with a question mark. Then, after the applicant leaves (or in the case of the practice activity, after you finish the exercise), go back to the question marks and think about the response and how to fit it into the rubric. You may find it helpful to underline key phrases in the rubric that were addressed in the response. The rating level that has more key phrases identified is the more appropriate rating.

The rubrics are different for each question. How realistic is it to use the protocol with real applicants?

The more familiar you are with the protocol and the rubrics, the more comfortable you will be rating applicants. The more you use the protocol, the easier it will be for you to classify responses according to the rubric. The actual interview form has space for taking notes about the response so you can mark your initial rating and then review your ratings after the applicant leaves, adjusting them if needed based on your notes and recollection of the interview responses.

How likely is it that I will identify exemplary applicants given the criteria of the rubric?

You are more likely to find that most applicants fall within the developing or proficient categories, but there will be those amazing applicants you cannot wait to hire. The criteria for an exemplary rating are stringent because such a rating incorporates all the facets of a proficient response and is even better. The reality is that we want the best teachers we can identify for our students. It is unrealistic to expect an applicant to score in the exemplary column on all questions. You may notice that you are rating an applicant as proficient most of the time, but that there are several exemplary ratings as well. You can identify trends in how an applicant responds and make a reasonable prediction that the applicant is likely a very effective teacher.

Teacher Quality Index Technical Information

The Teacher Quality Index is based on a synthesis of the extant research regarding the qualities of effective teachers as well as on research regarding selection interviews. The anchored rating scale used in the TQI protocol was validated through a national survey. The survey, which was sent to 300 practicing principals, collected information on building-level administrators' interviewing practices and their perceptions of statements associated with varying levels of teacher effectiveness. The level of agreement among administrators on how they rated statements, as well as the degree to which their ratings agreed with a research-based targeted rating, were summarized. Correlations and chi-square tests established that administrator demographics had little impact on how they rated a series of statements associated with teacher responses to interview questions. Here in Appendix A, we focus on the anchor rubric development. For the results of the complete study, see Hindman (2004).

Sample

A national, stratified, random sample of principals was used ($N = 300$). The sample was representative of the U.S. public school principalship population (see Figure A.1). Chi-square tests were used to compare the population, sample, and respondents; no statistical difference was found between the population, study sample, and usable respondents. The $x^2_{obs} = 3.28$ is less than $x^2_{crit} = 9.49$; thus, there is not a statistically significant interaction between the grade level and group. With alpha (α) equal to .05, a chi-square test on urban status is statistically significant, x^2 (4, $N = 86,713$) = 18.66, $p < .05$. There was an overrepresentation among rural respondents in the survey.

Of the usable surveys, respondents were all administrators with an average of 12.3 years of experience as an administrator, with a range from 1 to 44 years. Ninety-seven percent of respondents classified themselves as principals, while 2.8 percent classified themselves as other, which included superintendents who functioned as principals and assistant principals. More males (55.3 percent) responded than females (44.7 percent).

FIGURE A.1

Comparing the Population, Study Sample, and Usable Respondents

Variable	Population		Study Sample		Usable Respondents	
	N	%	*N*	%	*N*	%
School Level						
Elementary	67,800	68.7	206	68.7	82	61.7
Middle	14,300	14.5	44	14.7	25	18.8
High	16,543	16.8	50	16.7	26	19.5
Urban Status						
Urban	21,215	24.6	74	24.7	23	16.4
Suburban	39,768	46.1	138	46.0	53	37.9
Rural	25,290	29.3	88	29.3	64	45.7

Note: The totals for School Level and Urban Status are not the same because seven respondents reported working in settings that did not align cleanly as elementary, middle, or high school (i.e., K–8 or K–12).

Respondents worked in all six regions of the country: 8.5 percent Northeast, 11.3 percent Mid-Atlantic, 24.8 percent Southeast, 30.5 percent Central, 5.0 percent Southwest, and 19.9 percent Northwest.

Instrument Development

A survey instrument was developed that gathered participants' responses to questions on their demographics, interviewing practices, and perceptions of the strength of summary statements describing teacher applicants' responses to interview questions. The instrument was validated for use in this study.

Table of Specifications

A table of specifications was developed for the instrument to ensure that each of the qualities was represented among the questions (see Figure A.2). The qualities of effective teachers, as noted by Stronge (2002), are listed in

FIGURE A.2
Table of Specifications

Quality of Effective Teachers	# Items	Subcategory on the Teacher Effectiveness Behavior Scale
Personal Characteristics	3	Enthusiasm Caring; fairness and respect; positive relationships Reflection[a]
Classroom Management	2	Classroom organization Classroom management
Planning for Instruction	3	Planning, short- and long-term[a] Instructional complexity Time use
Instructional Delivery	4	Instructional differentiation Expectations for student learning Technology integration Instructional clarity
Assessment	2	Quality of feedback Assessment for understanding

[a]Items included in Stronge's (2002) framework but not explicitly identified as separate qualities.

the first column, and in the last column are the subcategories Stronge identified with each quality. For each question there were six associated response items for participants to rate as being associated with varying levels of teacher effectiveness.

Instrument Design

The 106-item Perceptions of School Leaders on Qualities of Effective Teachers Survey (see Appendix B) consisted of a combination of forced-choice responses and rating items. The survey also contained a strategic elimination question designed to remove individuals who had not conducted teacher interviews in the last year.

Specifically, Part I collected demographic and background information, Part II asked building-level administrators about their interviewing practices, and Part III solicited participants' association of summary statements of responses with the strength of that response based on the type of teacher applicant who would be likely to make such a statement. Specific verbal labels were selected to describe the type of teacher applicant in order to "clarify the meaning of the scale for participants" (Weisberg, Krosnick, & Bowen, 1996, p. 82). High-quality statements were considered exemplary, whereas low-quality statements were unsatisfactory. There were two middle levels: developing and proficient.

Instrument Validation: Pilot Studies

Two pilot studies were conducted to refine the instrument. The first established content validity between the proposed interview questions and the intended associated qualities of effective teachers. The second study collected feedback from practicing administrators on their perceptions of the intended rating of the level of teacher (i.e., unsatisfactory, developing, proficient, or exemplary) who would give the sample response to the question.

Piloting the Questions: Determination of Content Validity. Content validity measured the degree to which the questions relate to the specific quality of effective teaching (Weisberg et al., 1996). Adapting a protocol used by Bauer and colleagues (2001), a sample of school personnel familiar with the qualities of effective teachers ($N = 29$) sorted the questions back into subsections, and the proportion of correct matches was calculated. This was done to determine agreement between what the question was probing and how it was interpreted. The pilot respondents were asked about the alignment of the questions with the descriptions of qualities of effective teachers in order to establish content validity.

Item analysis was conducted to determine the variability of the responses. Items in which the majority of respondents agreed with the intended associated quality of an effective teacher were considered to have content validity.

Twenty-nine participants (100 percent participation and return) completed a two-page questionnaire exploring how qualities of effective teachers and interview questions were related. In 9 out of 14 questions, a majority of respondents associated the intended quality with the question.

In three of the situations where the respondents did not agree with the intended construct, they associated the question with a closely associated construct. The results of the pilot study indicated that respondents perceived a tight connection between "Organizing for Instruction" and "Instructional Delivery." Adjustments to the wording of the questions were made based on the data collected for the final survey instrument.

Piloting the Instrument: Determination of Reliability and Content Validity. In this second pilot study, respondents were asked to consider the responses associated with various levels of teacher effectiveness as opposed to the questions, which were the focus of the first pilot study. Content validity can be established by the consensus of individuals knowledgeable in the area (Gay, 1987; Litwin, 1995). The survey was reviewed with 13 practicing administrators to establish content validity. There were four elementary principals, five middle school administrators, and four high school administrators. The participants represented all three urban status classifications, with two serving in rural settings, five in suburban settings, and six in urban areas. Internal consistency was used as a measure of reliability. It was calculated at 0.7 using Spearman-Brown's formula, since the survey contained more than 50 items (Gay, 1987). Respondents agreed on the ratings provided based on the research literature 93 percent of the time, and within one level of the suggested rating 100 percent of the time.

The Study

The Perceptions of School Leaders on Qualities of Effective Teachers Survey (see Appendix B) had an overall response rate of 58.3 percent, of which 47.0 percent of the total responses were usable. The results of the study are organized around three questions:

1. To what extent is there consensus agreement among participants' rating of summary statements on the Perceptions of School Leaders on Qualities of Effective Teachers Survey?

2. To what extent is there agreement between a research-based rubric and participants' responses?

3. To what degree do participants' demographic characteristics (e.g., gender, school level, urban status, experience as an administrator, number of interviews conducted a year) relate to their association of statements with levels of teacher competence?

To what extent is there consensus agreement among participants' rating of summary statements on the Perceptions of School Leaders on Qualities of Effective Teachers Survey?

Respondents agreed on a rating for each statement by a simple majority for 75 out of 84 statements. In terms of the directionality of the ratings, there was an agreement of at least 75 percent of the respondents for a particular rating level plus or minus one level for all 84 statements (see Figure A.3, beginning on p. 105). In an exploratory study on teacher effectiveness, Stronge and colleagues (2003) found that being within one rating level was considered acceptable. In that study there were two observers, whereas the present study had up to 141 individuals providing independent ratings of statements. The implication is that being within plus or minus one rating level among the majority of respondents in a larger study is stronger than a close rating between two individuals.

To what extent is there agreement between a research-based rubric and participants' responses?

In general, respondents identified the research-based target for the response the majority of the time. Participants designated a level other than the research-based target for approximately one-quarter of the responses. However, in each of these cases, the preferred level was one level higher or lower than the target. Administrators were twice as likely to identify responses as one level lower than as one level higher than the target.

Figure A.3 contains boldfaced numbers indicating the percentage of respondents who agreed with the research-based target. As illustrated, this was the case 73.8 percent of the time, as shown by the targeted rating level receiving the highest percentage of responses. For 22 sample statements (26.2 percent), respondents selected a rating level other than the target.

The last two columns of the table in Figure A.3 illustrate how respondents rated the responses relative to the research-based target. The "primary" column indicates the level where most respondents associated a given response, while the column labeled "secondary" indicates the second most popular selection. The majority of the time, the research-based target and the administrators' majority response were in agreement, as indicated where the "primary" column is filled in with a 0. A plus or minus score in those columns indicates how many levels away from the research-based target a response was, with plus being above the target and minus being below. In a few cases, the majority of the administrators did not agree with the research-based target and were a level off, such that a +1 or −1 appears in the "primary" column. In two cases, the research-based target did not receive one of the two highest percentages of administrator agreement. A possible reason for the variation is that practicing administrators are influenced by the quality of applicants they encounter as opposed to studies that focus on specific variables of effectiveness.

To what degree do participants' demographic characteristics (e.g., gender, school level, urban status, experience as an administrator, number of interviews conducted a year) relate to their association of statements with levels of teacher competence?

Both chi-square tests and correlations were used to determine statistically significant relationships among participants' demographics and how they rated responses. Since school levels where administrators worked and urban status are discrete variables, chi-square tests were selected. The appendix following this section contains the wording of each question.

Levels. Chi-square tests were used to examine statistically significant interactions among the levels in which the administrators worked and the way they perceived the strength of the response. Sixteen of the statements showed statistically significant effects, as indicated in Figure A.4 (beginning on p. 110); however, the expected frequencies for all but one were less than 5. According to SPSS, the statistical program used, "some of the assumptions underlying the chi-square test are questionable in small samples, and statisticians commonly suggest a rule of thumb that all expected frequencies be at least 5 in order for the chi-square test to be considered reliable" (Kirkpatrick & Feeney, 2001, p. 105). This means that although the item was found to be statistically significant, due to the small number of responses in particular grade levels or rating levels, it may not show repeatable statistical significance if a larger sample were used resulting in larger cell sizes. One question (32C) met the criteria of both being statistically significant and having all expected cell sizes at least 5. The question dealt with instructional delivery, and administrators at the middle or high school level were more likely to identify the target response (71.4 percent and 63.0 percent, respectively) than elementary school principals, who rated the item one level higher (37.2 percent) or at target rating (40.8 percent).

Urban Status. In considering urban status (see Figure A.5, beginning on p. 112), it should be noted that rural respondents were overrepresented when compared to the population. This overrepresentation did not have an impact on the findings; while there were significant interactions, none of them passed the suggested rule of thumb of having expected cell sizes of at least 5. In general, the respondents' area (urban, suburban, rural) and the school level (elementary, middle, high) do not influence principals' perceptions of the strength of a response to a question. This is not surprising, because the questions were designed to be general and applicable to all working conditions. The potential for variability would have been increased if the questions or the associated responses were altered to favor practices or techniques more commonly found in particular settings. This finding of a lack of variability is encouraging in that it suggests that the interview questions and associated response items were not biased based on urban status or grade level.

Demographic Variables. Correlations were calculated on the variables of experience, number of interviews conducted, percent of novice teachers interviewed, and gender (see Figure A.6, beginning on p. 114). Based on the positive or negative correlation coefficients given, it is possible to determine the source of the influence. The methodology used in the study creates the possibility of finding correlations as so many were conducted. With an alpha (α) level of .05 selected, one would anticipate approximately 16 significant findings based on random chance, as 336 correlations were conducted.

Twenty-eight statistically significant correlations were identified across the four areas, which is more than can be attributed to random chance. Frequently, experience gained over time doing the same task or sheer repetition helps refine one's practice, making one more attuned to differences. Thus, it was anticipated that administrators with more years of experience or those who had conducted more interviews would be more likely to agree with the targeted ratings. Likewise, if principals interviewed higher percentages of novice teachers, it was assumed that their expectations would be lower, resulting in higher than anticipated ratings as they adjusted their expectations, yet the data did not support this assumption. The correlations associated with experience (5), number of interviews (1), and percent of novice applicants interviewed (3) can be attributed to chance, suggesting that the survey items were not influenced by these demographic factors. However, gender had 19 statistically significant correlations, indicating that more than just random chance is involved. In 17 out of 19 correlations, male administrators rated response items higher than female administrators, but the power of the correlations is small. With the exception of gender, demographic variables (e.g., grade level, urban status, experience, number of interviews, percent of novices interviewed) do not influence the ratings given on the survey.

Summary

The study targeted a specific element of a new teacher quality interview protocol that built upon extant effective teacher and interview research. The instrument designed for the protocol included many characteristics that the interview research base supports as good practice. The study validated the rubric portion of the interview protocol by extracting key phrases from it and embedding them in response statements to associated questions. Goals for the interview protocol include making better selection decisions, reducing turnover costs, and providing students with effective teachers. Using a rubric grounded in the effective teacher research literature will give administrators a tool to focus their evaluation of applicants' responses on qualities that have been empirically linked to higher levels of student achievement.

FIGURE A.3

Percentages of Respondents' Perception of Response Strength with Respect to Research-Based Targeted Response

Quality Domain/Items	Response Level				Response Selection Relative to Target	
	Unsatisfactory	Developing	Proficient	Exemplary	Primary	Secondary
Personal Characteristics						
23. What do you find most rewarding about teaching?						
a. Does not communicate his or her thoughts clearly	**83.5**	14.4	2.2	0	0	+1
b. Communicates with clarity and offers examples	0.7	7.2	**52.2**	39.9	0	+1
c. Communicates an idealistic but ungrounded view of teaching	13	**81.2**	5.1	0.7	0	−1
d. Communicates with useful concrete and abstract examples	0.7	8.1	50.7	**40.4**	−1	0
e. Communicates a broad idea that lacks specificity	9.4	**84.1**	5.8	0.7	0	−1
f. Communicates a passion for seeing students enjoying learning	0.7	16.1	34.3	**48.9**	0	−1
31. Give an example of how you establish and maintain a rapport with your students.						
a. Watches TV shows that are popular with students	60.7	**35.0**	3.6	0.7	−1	0
b. Provides examples of caring about individual students in and out of school	0.7	12.9	51.4	**35.0**	−1	0
c. Says it is hard to relate to students who are so different from the teacher or other students he or she has taught	**87.9**	10.7	1.4	0	0	+1
d. Focuses on the teacher role of controlling students	**55.7**	38.6	5.7	0	0	+1
e. Offers examples of involvement with students outside of contract hours (e.g., club, coaching, attendance at extracurricular events)	0	8.0	50.0	**42.0**	−1	0
f. Interacts and knows students by group interests	0	13.7	**59.7**	26.6	0	+1
36. Think about a lesson that did not meet your expectations, despite planning and preparation. Tell me what you considered when planning to readdress the topic with your students and describe how you altered your approach.						
a. Focuses on non-teacher-related issues	**70.0**	26.4	3.6	0	0	+1
b. Addresses the issue with limited evidence of reflection	34.5	**64.0**	1.4	0	0	−1
c. Reflects to improve teaching	0	22.1	**65.7**	12.1	0	−1
d. Reflects on the teaching and the students to improve learning	0	2.2	38.1	**59.7**	0	−1
e. Focuses on what the students did wrong	**54.3**	39.3	5.7	0.7	0	+1
f. Describes reteaching the concept another way so students could learn	0.7	9.9	**50.4**	39.0	0	+1

Note: Bold type indicates targeted response based on the effective teacher research. "Primary" refers to the rating selected most often; "Secondary" refers to the second most fequent selection.

Scale for primary and secondary response selection: 0 = Target   +1 = One level above target   +2 = Two levels above target   −1 = One level below target   −2 = Two levels below target

FIGURE A.3

Percentages of Respondents' Perception of Response Strength with Respect to Research-Based Targeted Response (*continued*)

Quality Domain/Items	Response Level				Response Selection Relative to Target	
	Unsatisfactory	Developing	Proficient	Exemplary	Primary	Secondary
Classroom Management						
24. Tell me what you do with students during the first few weeks of the school year to establish a positive classroom environment.						
a. Builds a classroom community through student ownership	0.7	5.8	40.6	**52.9**	0	−1
b. Offers limited opportunities for students to practice routines	50.4	**45.3**	0.7	3.6	−1	0
c. Lacks specific examples of how they build rapport with students	**73.9**	23.2	2.2	0.7	0	+1
d. Introduces rules only once and expects students to follow them	**75.9**	21.9	2.2	0	0	+1
e. Spends time at the start of the school year reinforcing routines so students can work independently	0.7	10.8	**54.0**	34.5	0	+1
f. Responds to students who are off task and redirects them	1.7	22.5	**54.3**	21.7	0	−1
27. Share with me a time you had difficulty with a particular student's behavior and what you did to address it.						
a. Works with the student and others (e.g., families, guidance counselors) to help the student meet expectations	0	2.9	48.2	**48.9**	0	−1
b. Disciplines students using punitive measures	**56.5**	37.0	5.8	0.7	0	+1
c. Focuses on the need for strict discipline measures	38.1	**55.4**	6.5	0	0	−1
d. Reinforces the behavior expectations	2.2	24.1	**62.4**	9.5	0	−1
e. Refers the student to the office if he or she does not improve during the class period	**30.9**	58.3	10.1	0.7	+1	0
f. Provides an example where a contributing factor was the teacher's actions	12.6	**28.1**	47.4	11.9	+1	0
Planning for Instruction						
25. Share with me your long- and short-term planning process.						
a. Treats long- and short-term planning as isolated planning functions	36.2	**59.4**	4.3	0	0	−1
b. Does not make long-range plans or is unfamiliar with the concept	**84.9**	14.4	0.7	0	0	+1
c. Prioritizes instruction by referring to plans	1.4	34.5	56.1	**7.9**	−1	−2
d. Uses both long- and short-term planning, relying heavily on short-term	0.7	39.3	**50.7**	9.3	0	1
e. Uses planning to help consolidate facts into broader concepts	0	10.9	61.3	**27.7**	−1	0
f. Indicates that long-range planning is not useful as there are too many interruptions in the school year	**79.1**	17.3	2.9	0.7	0	+1

FIGURE A.3

Percentages of Respondents' Perception of Response Strength with Respect to Research-Based Targeted Response (*continued*)

	Response Level				Response Selection Relative to Target	
Quality Domain/Items	Unsatisfactory	Developing	Proficient	Exemplary	Primary	Secondary
29. Think about a unit you have taught. Tell me why you selected particular teaching strategies to address the curriculum.						
a. Diagnostically uses a wide range of instructional strategies to optimize student learning	0	1.4	25.2	**73.4**	0	−1
b. Refers to a few instructional strategies he or she knows well	15.8	**74.1**	10.1	0	0	−1
c. Selects strategies that appeal to students' learning styles	0.7	8.6	**72.7**	18.0	0	+1
d. Considers the resources available to teach using various strategies	0.7	30.2	**56.1**	12.9	0	−1
e. Works with another teacher who suggested the strategies would work well to teach the unit to students	2.9	**51.4**	37.9	7.9	0	+1
f. Credits the textbook with the selection of strategies	**42.4**	54.7	2.9	0	−1	0
33. How does your use of instructional time demonstrate that learning is students' primary focus?						
a. Focuses on how learning time may be interrupted by external events, so the teacher verbally reminds students to pay attention	**28.3**	60.9	10.9	0	+1	0
b. Talks about cutting short lessons because noninstructional activities use up the time	**77.7**	20.1	2.2	0	0	+1
c. Considers the time it takes the educator to teach and the students to learn when allocating time	3.6	21.6	**58.3**	16.5	0	−1
d. Offers examples of how a high percentage of the day is devoted to instruction, such as taking advantage of teachable moments	0	2.9	47.5	**49.6**	0	−1
e. Gives a basic answer about how much time is spent in class	**24.5**	71.9	3.6	0	+1	0
f. Is flexible in time use to ensure students learn	0	7.9	**65.5**	26.6	0	+1
Instructional Delivery						
26. Describe how you engage students in their learning.						
a. Modifies activities to address student needs	0	5.7	**63.6**	30.7	0	+1
b. Systematically designs differentiated learning activities	0	1.4	30.5	**68.1**	0	−1
c. Has a "one size fits all" approach to instruction	**80.4**	18.1	0.7	0.7	0	+1
d. Provides some activities designed to capitalize on student interest	0.7	**70.3**	25.4	3.6	0	+1
e. Provides examples of how he or she achieves high levels of active student engagement	0	6.5	50.0	**43.5**	−1	0
f. Does not think school should have to cater to student interests	**96.4**	2.2	1.4	0	0	+1

FIGURE A.3

Percentages of Respondents' Perception of Response Strength with Respect to Research-Based Targeted Response (*continued*)

Quality Domain/Items	Response Level				Response Selection Relative to Target	
	Unsatisfactory	Developing	Proficient	Exemplary	Primary	Secondary
32. Describe how you promote high expectations for student achievement during your instructional time.						
a. Offers examples of what meeting varying levels of expectation looks like on particular assignments	0	2.9	43.2	**54**	0	−1
b. Is enthusiastic about learning	0.7	**23.2**	42.0	34.1	+1	+2
c. Encourages students to participate in their learning	20.9	**51.8**	27.3	0	0	+1
d. Places sole responsibility for student success on the student	**68.3**	26.6	5	0	0	+1
e. Believes that different students have different needs at different times, so high expectations reflect student differences	5.8	12.2	44.6	**37.4**	−1	0
f. Suggests that student achievement is the job of the student and is influenced slightly by the teacher	**64.0**	32.4	3.6	0	0	+1
34. How do you use technology as part of your instruction?						
a. Offers examples of how technology and other related resources are integrated into meaningful lessons	0.7	2.1	38.6	**58.6**	0	−1
b. Is uncomfortable with technology	**72.9**	21.4	3.6	2.1	0	+1
c. Creates tasks to increase students' proficiency and expertise in appropriately using the technology	0.7	6.5	59.0	**33.8**	−1	0
d. Uses available technology as appropriate to instructional objectives	0.7	17.1	**67.1**	15.0	0	−1
e. Applies technology inappropriately in the example	70.7	**23.6**	4.3	1.4	−1	0
f. Fails to provide an example of authentic student work using technology	**77.0**	21.6	0.7	0.7	0	+1
35. Pick a topic in your subject area that is often difficult for students to understand. Tell me what the topic is and how you explain it to students, and share with me directions for an activity you do to help further students' understanding of that topic.						
a. Provides an inadequate answer that demonstrates some knowledge	**48.6**	47.1	4.3	0	0	+1
b. Offers plentiful instructional examples and guided practice	0	2.9	56.8	**40.3**	−1	0
c. Gives confusing examples and directions in the example selected	**74.3**	24.3	1.4	0	0	+1
d. Communicates the topic with a lack of clarity	**48.9**	46.8	3.6	0.7	0	+1
e. Provides an example in which the class was addressed as a group on the topic and then the teacher targeted specific individuals for additional explanation as necessary	1.4	22.1	52.1	**24.3**	−1	0
f. Uses clear examples and step-by-step directions	0	3.6	**61.4**	35.0	0	+1

Percentages of Respondents' Perception of Response Strength with Respect to Research-Based Targeted Response (*continued*)

Quality Domain/Items	Response Level				Response Selection Relative to Target	
	Unsatisfactory	Developing	Proficient	Exemplary	Primary	Secondary
Assessment						
28. Explain how you share your grading system with students and families.						
a. Uses a limited variety of ongoing and culminating assessments	9.4	**66.9**	14.4	9.4	0	+1
b. Grades a variety of assignments and more formal assessments	0.7	24.5	**66.9**	7.9	0	−1
c. Has a mechanism in place for explaining the grading system when new students enter the class during the year (e.g., a welcome pack)	1.4	13.0	55.8	**29.7**	−1	0
d. Provides adequate feedback on performance	1.5	27.0	**63.5**	8.0	0	−1
e. Interprets and communicates student progress through regularly timed reports that are issued in addition to the school's marking period	0	2.9	35.7	**61.4**	0	-1
f. Prefers to base grades solely on culminating assignments (e.g., tests)	**53.2**	43.9	1.4	1.4	0	+1
30. Tell me how you accommodate students' learning needs in the assessments you give.						
a. Analyzes past student performance on assessments to determine how the student best demonstrates his or her knowledge	0	10.8	44.6	**44.6**	Tied 0/−1	Tied 0/−1
b. Assesses all students the same	59.4	**37.7**	2.9	0	−1	0
c. Gives modified assessments when they are prepared by the special education teacher	13.7	**53.2**	30.2	2.9	0	+1
d. Differentiates as appropriate for students of all ability levels	0	3.5	40.4	**56.0**	0	−1
e. Changes some aspects of the assessment based on the instruction students received	2.1	39.3	**46.4**	12.1	0	−1
f. Accommodates only when there is an IEP or 504 plan being enforced	**62.1**	34.3	3.6	0	0	+1

FIGURE A.4
Level and Question Response

Question[a]	N	x^2_{obs}	df[b]	Asymptotic Significance[c] (2-Sided)
23A	131	15.132	4	.004**
23B	129	1.865	6	.932
23C	130	4.797	6	.570
23D	128	5.995	6	.424
23E	130	3.613	6	.729
23F	130	5.637	6	.465
24A	129	2.258	6	.895
24B	131	4.208	6	.649
24C	130	12.958	6	.044*
24D	129	16.261	4	.003**
24E	131	6.429	6	.377
24F	130	2.604	6	.857
25A	130	3.503	4	.477
25B	131	8.885	4	.064
25C	131	4.352	6	.629
25D	131	3.972	6	.680
25E	129	2.429	4	.657
25F	131	13.744	6	.033*
26A	132	2.288	4	.683
26B	132	3.899	4	.420
26C	131	14.834	6	.022*
26D	130	5.537	6	.477
26E	130	2.683	4	.612
26F	131	10.825	4	.029*
27A	130	.810	4	.937
27B	130	16.188	6	.013*
27C	131	.631	4	.960
27D	129	5.988	6	.425
27E	130	8.779	4	.067
27F	128	7.451	6	.281
28A	131	4.497	6	.610
28B	131	7.576	6	.271
28C	130	4.920	6	.554
28D	129	6.951	6	.325
28E	131	4.312	4	.365
28F	131	3.452	6	.750
29A	130	4.507	4	.342
29B	131	1.097	4	.895
29C	131	5.888	6	.436
29D	131	13.768	6	.032*
29E	131	6.350	6	.385
29F	131	4.159	4	.385

[a]See Appendix B for the wording of each question.
[b]Degrees of freedom differ due to some items in which a possible response was not selected by any of the survey respondents.
[c]"Asymptotic" means that the tails of a normal distribution come close to the baseline, but never touch it.

*$\alpha = .05$ $df = 4$, $x^2_{crit} = 9.49$ $df = 6$, $x^2_{crit} = 12.6$
**$\alpha = .01$ $df = 4$, $x^2_{crit} = 13.3$ $df = 6$, $x^2_{crit} = 16.8$

FIGURE A.4
Level and Question Response (*continued*)

Question[a]	N	x^2_{obs}	df[b]	Asymptotic Significance[c] (2-Sided)
30A	131	5.465	4	.243
30B	130	1.359	4	.851
30C	131	7.836	6	.250
30D	132	7.125	4	.129
30E	132	2.622	6	.855
30F	132	14.074	4	.007**
31A	132	9.111	6	.167
31B	132	6.300	6	.390
31C	132	3.783	4	.436
31D	132	9.450	4	.051
31E	130	2.217	4	.696
31F	130	3.985	4	.408
32A	131	4.126	4	.389
32B	130	3.167	6	.788
32C	131	11.108	4	.025*
32D	131	5.059	4	.281
32E	130	9.426	6	.151
32F	131	2.373	4	.668
33A	130	15.672	4	.003**
33B	131	9.478	4	.050
33C	131	6.147	6	.407
33D	131	15.201	4	.004**
33E	131	6.680	4	.154
33F	130	2.289	4	.683
34A	131	11.874	6	.065
34B	132	5.667	6	.461
34C	132	1.830	6	.935
34D	132	5.718	6	.456
34E	132	10.285	6	.113
34F	131	7.282	6	.296
35A	132	11.701	4	.020*
35B	131	.516	4	.972
35C	132	10.104	4	.039*
35D	131	7.237	6	.299
35E	131	5.734	6	.454
35F	132	4.430	4	.351
36A	132	11.347	4	.023*
36B	131	10.419	4	.034*
36C	132	6.511	4	.164
36D	131	2.365	4	.669
36E	132	8.071	6	.233
36F	132	3.380	6	.760

[a]See Appendix B for the wording of each question.

[b]Degrees of freedom differ due to some items in which a possible response was not selected by any of the survey respondents.

[c]"Asymptotic" means that the tails of a normal distribution come close to the baseline, but never touch it.

*$\alpha = .05$ $df = 4$, $x^2_{crit} = 9.49$ $df = 6$, $x^2_{crit} = 12.6$

**$\alpha = .01$ $df = 4$, $x^2_{crit} = 13.3$ $df = 6$, $x^2_{crit} = 16.8$

FIGURE A.5
Urban Status and Question Response

Question[a]	N	x^2_{obs}	df[b]	Asymptotic Significance[c] (2-Sided)
23A	138	4.086	4	.395
23B	137	11.495	6	.074
23C	137	1.457	6	.962
23D	135	4.021	6	.674
23E	137	2.298	6	.812
23F	136	6.520	6	.368
24A	137	6.712	6	.348
24B	138	4.544	6	.603
24C	137	8.628	6	.196
24D	136	3.144	4	.534
24E	138	9.832	6	.132
24F	137	8.357	6	.213
25A	137	5.671	4	.225
25B	138	7.196	4	.126
25C	138	5.410	6	.492
25D	139	5.295	6	.507
25E	136	5.525	4	.238
25F	138	5.249	6	.512
26A	139	1.120	4	.891
26B	140	4.224	4	.376
26C	137	6.241	6	.367
26D	137	3.947	6	.684
26E	137	4.000	4	.364
26F	138	13.712	4	.008**
27A	138	1.526	4	.822
27B	137	14.567	6	.024*
27C	138	16.048	4	.003**
27D	136	5.971	6	.426
27E	138	13.170	6	.040*
27F	134	2.542	6	.864
28A	138	3.301	6	.770
28B	138	7.666	6	.264
28C	137	3.489	6	.745
28D	136	4.396	6	.623
28E	139	3.159	4	.532
28F	138	5.054	6	.537
29A	138	3.449	4	.486
29B	138	3.216	4	.522
29C	138	.618	4	.961
29D	138	3.074	6	.799
29E	139	6.047	6	.418
29F	138	2.887	4	.577

[a]See Appendix B for the wording of each question.

[b]Degrees of freedom differ due to some items in which a possible response was not selected by any of the survey respondents.

[c]"Asymptotic" means that the tails of a normal distribution come close to the baseline, but never touch it.

*$\alpha = .05$ $df = 4$, $x^2_{crit} = 9.49$ $df = 6$, $x^2_{crit} = 12.6$

**$\alpha = .01$ $df = 4$, $x^2_{crit} = 13.3$ $df = 6$, $x^2_{crit} = 16.8$

FIGURE A.5
Urban Status and Question Response (*continued*)

Question[a]	N	x^2_{obs}	df[b]	Asymptotic Significance[c] (2-Sided)
30A	138	9.581	4	.048*
30B	137	5.837	4	.212
30C	138	5.153	6	.524
30D	140	4.774	4	.311
30E	139	12.044	6	.061
30F	139	5.767	4	.217
31A	139	10.512	6	.015
31B	139	4.900	6	.557
31C	139	4.104	4	.392
31D	139	6.210	4	.184
31E	137	1.552	4	.817
31F	138	2.475	4	.649
32A	138	6.423	4	.490
32B	137	5.061	6	.536
32C	138	3.806	4	.433
32D	138	1.359	4	.851
32E	138	1.099	6	.982
32F	138	10.601	4	.031*
33A	137	2.494	4	.646
33B	138	7.986	4	.092
33C	138	3.360	6	.763
33D	138	4.345	4	.361
33E	138	6.189	4	.185
33F	138	3.323	4	.505
34A	139	9.958	6	.126
34B	139	10.734	6	.097
34C	138	3.444	6	.751
34D	139	2.676	6	.848
34E	139	13.269	6	.039*
34F	138	8.445	6	.207
35A	139	3.361	4	.499
35B	138	6.239	4	.182
35C	139	3.962	4	.411
35D	138	6.014	6	.422
35E	139	4.747	6	.577
35F	139	.763	4	.943
36A	139	4.017	4	.404
36B	138	13.452	4	.009**
36C	139	5.637	4	.228
36D	138	5.343	4	.254
36E	139	6.433	6	.376
36F	140	5.001	6	.544

[a]See Appendix B for the wording of each question.
[b]Degrees of freedom differ due to some items in which a possible response was not selected by any of the survey respondents.
[c]"Asymptotic" means that the tails of a normal distribution come close to the baseline, but never touch it.

*$\alpha = .05$ $df = 4$, $x^2_{crit} = 9.49$ $df = 6$, $x^2_{crit} = 12.6$
**$\alpha = .01$ $df = 4$, $x^2_{crit} = 13.3$ $df = 6$, $x^2_{crit} = 16.8$

FIGURE A.6
Correlations of Respondents' Demographics and Associations of Statements of Teacher Effectiveness

Question[a]		Experience	Number of Interviews Conducted	% of Novices Interviewed	Gender
PC23A	Pearson correlation	−0.114	0.047	0.017	0.168*
	sig. (2-tailed)	0.183	0.586	0.845	0.049
	N	138	139	139	138
PC23B	Pearson correlation	−0.106	−0.041	−0.109	−0.181*
	sig. (2-tailed)	0.219	0.633	0.204	0.034
	N	137	138	138	137
PC23C	Pearson correlation	0.025	0.103	−0.010	0.260**
	sig. (2-tailed)	0.769	0.231	0.910	0.002
	N	137	138	138	137
PC23D	Pearson correlation	0.056	0.032	−0.041	0.107
	sig. (2-tailed)	0.520	0.711	0.638	0.216
	N	135	136	136	135
PC23E	Pearson correlation	0.077	−0.068	−0.065	0.023
	sig. (2-tailed)	0.370	0.425	0.445	0.791
	N	137	138	138	137
PC23F	Pearson correlation	0.082	−0.024	0.030	0.058
	sig. (2-tailed)	0.345	0.777	0.727	0.506
	N	136	137	137	136
CM24A	Pearson correlation	0.085	0.050	−0.063	−0.211*
	sig. (2-tailed)	0.321	0.557	0.464	0.013
	N	137	138	138	137
CM24B	Pearson correlation	0.001	−0.066	−0.101	0.083
	sig. (2-tailed)	0.994	0.439	0.235	0.334
	N	138	139	139	138
CM24C	Pearson correlation	0.024	−0.048	0.011	0.195*
	sig. (2-tailed)	0.784	0.575	0.897	0.022
	N	137	138	138	137
CM24D	Pearson correlation	0.153	−0.022	0.080	0.186*
	sig. (2-tailed)	0.075	0.798	0.351	0.030
	N	136	137	137	136
CM24E	Pearson correlation	0.046	0.086	0.093	0.014
	sig. (2-tailed)	0.590	0.316	0.274	0.875
	N	138	139	139	138
CM24F	Pearson correlation	−0.091	−0.010	0.114	−0.037
	sig. (2-tailed)	0.292	0.907	0.183	0.671
	N	137	138	138	137

Note: PC = Personal characteristics   CM = Classroom management   OI = Organizing for instruction   ID = Instructional delivery   A = Assessment
[a]The wording of each question can be found in Appendix B.
*$p < .05$ **$p < .01$

FIGURE A.6
Correlations of Respondents' Demographics and
Associations of Statements of Teacher Effectiveness (*continued*)

Question[a]		Experience	Number of Interviews Conducted	% of Novices Interviewed	Gender
OI25A	Pearson correlation	−0.098	0.029	0.030	0.049
	sig. (2-tailed)	0.253	0.732	0.723	0.566
	N	137	138	138	137
OI25B	Pearson correlation	−0.021	0.019	0.001	0.179*
	sig. (2-tailed)	0.808	0.827	0.993	0.036
	N	138	139	139	138
OI25C	Pearson correlation	−0.014	0.084	0.092	0.077
	sig. (2-tailed)	0.873	0.326	0.283	0.369
	N	138	139	139	138
OI25D	Pearson correlation	0.210	−0.040	0.005	0.188*
	sig. (2-tailed)	0.013	0.641	0.955	0.027
	N	139	140	140	139
OI25E	Pearson correlation	−0.008	0.145	0.044	0.057
	sig. (2-tailed)	0.926	0.090	0.610	0.510
	N	136	137	137	136
OI25F	Pearson correlation	−0.004	−0.047	0.003	0.256**
	sig. (2-tailed)	0.962	0.583	0.976	0.002
	N	138	139	139	138
ID26A	Pearson correlation	0.062	0.108	0.042	0.009
	sig. (2-tailed)	0.471	0.206	0.622	0.912
	N	139	140	140	139
ID26B	Pearson correlation	0.085	0.100	−0.061	−0.126
	sig. (2-tailed)	0.316	0.237	0.470	0.138
	N	140	141	141	140
ID26C	Pearson correlation	0.037	0.113	0.109	0.189*
	sig. (2-tailed)	0.668	0.187	0.204	0.027
	N	137	138	138	137
ID26D	Pearson correlation	−0.023	−0.053	−0.168*	0.095
	sig. (2-tailed)	0.786	0.533	0.049	0.267
	N	137	138	138	137
ID26E	Pearson correlation	−0.012	0.018	−0.053	−0.089
	sig. (2-tailed)	0.893	0.838	0.535	0.300
	N	137	138	138	137
ID26F	Pearson correlation	0.005	0.085	−0.062	0.163
	sig. (2-tailed)	0.949	0.322	0.465	0.057
	N	138	139	139	138

Note: PC = Personal characteristics   CM = Classroom management   OI = Organizing for instruction   ID = Instructional delivery   A = Assessment
[a]The wording of each question can be found in Appendix B.
*$p < .05$ **$p < .01$

FIGURE A.6
Correlations of Respondents' Demographics and
Associations of Statements of Teacher Effectiveness (*continued*)

Question[a]		Experience	Number of Interviews Conducted	% of Novices Interviewed	Gender
CM27A	Pearson correlation	−0.027	−0.008	0.048	−0.085
	sig. (2-tailed)	0.751	0.930	0.576	0.319
	N	138	139	139	138
CM27B	Pearson correlation	0.004	−0.055	0.082	0.154
	sig. (2-tailed)	0.966	0.525	0.338	0.072
	N	137	138	138	137
CM27C	Pearson correlation	0.065	−0.057	0.002	0.223
	sig. (2-tailed)	0.447	0.507	0.983	0.008
	N	138	139	139	138
CM27D	Pearson correlation	0.008	−0.083	0.176*	0.055
	sig. (2-tailed)	0.927	0.337	0.040	0.522
	N	136	137	137	136
CM27E	Pearson correlation	0.183*	0.007	0.091	−0.026
	sig. (2-tailed)	0.032	0.933	0.284	0.763
	N	138	139	139	138
CM27F	Pearson correlation	−0.058	−0.058	0.086	0.014
	sig. (2-tailed)	0.508	0.506	0.323	0.875
	N	134	135	135	134
A28A	Pearson correlation	0.037	0.008	0.090	−0.067
	sig. (2-tailed)	0.669	0.925	0.295	0.438
	N	138	139	139	138
A28B	Pearson correlation	−0.185*	0.037	0.155	−0.068
	sig. (2-tailed)	0.030	0.668	0.069	0.431
	N	138	139	139	138
A28C	Pearson correlation	−0.047	−0.005	0.092	0.096
	sig. (2-tailed)	0.584	0.949	0.285	0.267
	N	137	138	138	137
A28D	Pearson correlation	−0.017	−0.120	0.054	−0.006
	sig. (2-tailed)	0.843	0.162	0.533	0.947
	N	136	137	137	136
A28E	Pearson correlation	0.107	−0.012	0.128	0.095
	sig. (2-tailed)	0.210	0.885	0.131	0.268
	N	139	140	140	139
A28F	Pearson correlation	0.033	−0.015	0.044	0.058
	sig. (2-tailed)	0.699	0.858	0.606	0.503
	N	138	139	139	138

Note: PC = Personal characteristics   CM = Classroom management   OI = Organizing for instruction   ID = Instructional delivery   A = Assessment
[a]The wording of each question can be found in Appendix B.
*$p < .05$ **$p < .01$

FIGURE A.6

Correlations of Respondents' Demographics and
Associations of Statements of Teacher Effectiveness (*continued*)

Question[a]		Experience	Number of Interviews Conducted	% of Novices Interviewed	Gender
OI29A	Pearson correlation	0.022	0.118	−0.047	-0.146
	sig. (2-tailed)	0.797	0.167	0.581	0.087
	N	138	139	139	138
OI29B	Pearson correlation	0.118	0.079	0.003	0.071
	sig. (2-tailed)	0.169	0.358	0.970	0.409
	N	138	139	139	138
OI29C	Pearson correlation	0.079	−0.161	−0.058	0.077
	sig. (2-tailed)	0.355	0.058	0.494	0.367
	N	138	139	139	138
OI29D	Pearson correlation	0.016	−0.046	−0.066	−0.078
	sig. (2-tailed)	0.852	0.590	0.443	0.364
	N	138	139	139	138
OI29E	Pearson correlation	−0.001	−0.286**	−0.026	0.035
	sig. (2-tailed)	0.992	0.001	0.762	0.679
	N	139	140	140	139
OI29F	Pearson correlation	0.035	−0.164	0.079	0.206*
	sig. (2-tailed)	0.687	0.054	0.357	0.016
	N	138	139	139	138
A30A	Pearson correlation	0.092	0.089	−0.051	0.032
	sig. (2-tailed)	0.281	0.295	0.548	0.713
	N	138	139	139	138
A30B	Pearson correlation	0.045	−0.072	−0.080	0.061
	sig. (2-tailed)	0.604	0.404	0.349	0.481
	N	137	138	138	137
A30C	Pearson correlation	0.014	0.137	0.052	0.169*
	sig. (2-tailed)	0.871	0.107	0.545	0.048
	N	138	139	139	138
A30D	Pearson correlation	0.051	0.087	−0.119	−0.006
	sig. (2-tailed)	0.552	0.305	0.161	0.946
	N	140	141	141	140
A30E	Pearson correlation	−0.029	−0.045	0.019	−0.038
	sig. (2-tailed)	0.731	0.594	0.825	0.654
	N	139	140	140	139
A30F	Pearson correlation	−0.125	−0.130	0.044	0.038
	sig. (2-tailed)	0.142	0.126	0.606	0.661
	N	139	140	140	139

Note: PC = Personal characteristics   CM = Classroom management   OI = Organizing for instruction   ID = Instructional delivery   A = Assessment
[a]The wording of each question can be found in Appendix B.
*$p < .05$ **$p < .01$

FIGURE A.6
Correlations of Respondents' Demographics and Associations of Statements of Teacher Effectiveness (*continued*)

Question[a]		Experience	Number of Interviews Conducted	% of Novices Interviewed	Gender
PC31A	Pearson correlation	0.031	0.105	0.044	0.029
	sig. (2-tailed)	0.717	0.215	0.602	0.734
	N	139	140	140	139
PC31B	Pearson correlation	−0.008	0.016	0.007	−0.112
	sig. (2-tailed)	0.922	0.852	0.937	0.190
	N	139	140	140	139
PC31C	Pearson correlation	0.048	−0.108	0.012	0.126
	sig. (2-tailed)	0.575	0.205	0.887	0.138
	N	139	140	140	139
PC31D	Pearson correlation	0.123	−0.039	0.077	0.209*
	sig. (2-tailed)	0.148	0.646	0.368	0.013
	N	139	140	140	139
PC31E	Pearson correlation	0.049	0.098	−0.056	−0.049
	sig. (2-tailed)	0.573	0.253	0.515	0.570
	N	137	138	138	137
PC31F	Pearson correlation	−0.005	−0.008	−0.006	−0.118
	sig. (2-tailed)	0.954	0.924	0.948	0.168
	N	138	139	139	138
ID32A	Pearson correlation	0.076	−0.025	0.006	−0.003
	sig. (2-tailed)	0.375	0.766	0.944	0.968
	N	138	139	139	138
ID32B	Pearson correlation	−0.035	−0.105	0.050	0.032
	sig. (2-tailed)	0.686	0.219	0.558	0.708
	N	137	138	138	137
ID32C	Pearson correlation	0.008	−0.024	0.029	0.019
	sig. (2-tailed)	0.924	0.775	0.737	0.823
	N	138	139	139	138
ID32D	Pearson correlation	−0.080	−0.011	−0.074	−0.021
	sig. (2-tailed)	0.353	0.899	0.389	0.808
	N	138	139	139	138
ID32E	Pearson correlation	0.168*	0.021	0.022	0.041
	sig. (2-tailed)	0.049	0.807	0.793	0.629
	N	138	139	139	138
ID32F	Pearson correlation	−0.056	−0.038	0.057	−0.014
	sig. (2-tailed)	0.511	0.656	0.506	0.873
	N	138	139	139	138

Note: PC = Personal characteristics   CM = Classroom management   OI = Organizing for instruction   ID = Instructional delivery   A = Assessment
[a]The wording of each question can be found in Appendix B.
*$p < .05$ **$p < .01$

FIGURE A.6
Correlations of Respondents' Demographics and
Associations of Statements of Teacher Effectiveness (*continued*)

Question[a]		Experience	Number of Interviews Conducted	% of Novices Interviewed	Gender
OI33A	Pearson correlation	0.122	0.088	−0.040	0.183*
	sig. (2-tailed)	0.157	0.304	0.641	0.033
	N	137	138	138	137
OI33B	Pearson correlation	0.051	0.105	0.067	0.177*
	sig. (2–tailed)	0.554	0.218	0.434	0.038
	N	138	139	139	138
OI33C	Pearson correlation	0.011	−0.105	0.044	0.010
	sig. (2-tailed)	0.897	0.219	0.607	0.908
	N	138	139	139	138
OI33D	Pearson correlation	−0.061	0.041	0.085	−0.125
	sig. (2-tailed)	0.478	0.629	0.322	0.144
	N	138	139	139	138
OI33E	Pearson correlation	0.075	−0.147	0.183*	0.221**
	sig. (2-tailed)	0.385	0.085	0.031	0.009
	N	138	139	139	138
OI33F	Pearson correlation	−0.028	−0.166	0.087	−0.065
	sig. (2-tailed)	0.741	0.050	0.306	0.446
	N	138	139	139	138
ID34A	Pearson correlation	0.168	−0.083	0.061	0.009
	sig. (2-tailed)	0.048	0.331	0.477	0.919
	N	139	140	140	139
ID34B	Pearson correlation	0.077	−0.056	0.007	0.068
	sig. (2-tailed)	0.365	0.513	0.934	0.427
	N	139	140	140	139
ID34C	Pearson correlation	0.000	−0.088	−0.044	−0.050
	sig. (2-tailed)	0.999	0.304	0.609	0.558
	N	138	139	139	138
ID34D	Pearson correlation	−0.075	−0.076	−0.004	−0.127
	sig. (2-tailed)	0.378	0.372	0.959	0.136
	N	139	140	140	139
ID34E	Pearson correlation	0.004	−0.047	0.090	0.067
	sig. (2-tailed)	0.961	0.582	0.291	0.432
	N	139	140	140	139
ID34F	Pearson correlation	−0.020	−0.056	−0.086	0.043
	sig. (2-tailed)	0.818	0.513	0.316	0.615
	N	138	139	139	138

Note: PC = Personal characteristics   CM = Classroom management   OI = Organizing for instruction   ID = Instructional delivery   A = Assessment
[a]The wording of each question can be found in Appendix B.
*$p < .05$ **$p < .01$

FIGURE A.6
Correlations of Respondents' Demographics and
Associations of Statements of Teacher Effectiveness (*continued*)

Question[a]		Experience	Number of Interviews Conducted	% of Novices Interviewed	Gender
ID35A	Pearson correlation	−0.082	−0.061	0.034	0.070
	sig. (2-tailed)	0.340	0.476	0.691	0.412
	N	139	140	140	139
ID35B	Pearson correlation	0.066	0.094	−0.026	0.152
	sig. (2-tailed)	0.445	0.272	0.758	0.076
	N	138	139	139	138
ID35C	Pearson correlation	0.251*	−0.014	−0.002	0.173*
	sig. (2-tailed)	0.003	0.870	0.980	0.042
	N	139	140	140	139
ID35D	Pearson correlation	−0.047	−0.033	0.140	0.192*
	sig. (2-tailed)	0.587	0.702	0.100	0.024
	N	138	139	139	138
ID35E	Pearson correlation	−0.103	−0.162	0.092	−0.089
	sig. (2-tailed)	0.229	0.056	0.281	0.299
	N	139	140	140	139
ID35F	Pearson correlation	0.143	−0.028	0.004	0.116
	sig. (2-tailed)	0.093	0.740	0.964	0.173
	N	139	140	140	139
PC36A	Pearson correlation	0.124	−0.062	0.073	0.230**
	sig. (2-tailed)	0.146	0.468	0.392	0.006
	N	139	140	140	139
PC36B	Pearson correlation	0.110	−0.080	0.014	0.091
	sig. (2-tailed)	0.200	0.349	0.869	0.289
	N	138	139	139	138
PC36C	Pearson correlation	0.032	0.084	−0.066	0.122
	sig. (2-tailed)	0.709	0.326	0.439	0.154
	N	139	140	140	139
PC36D	Pearson correlation	−0.120	0.004	0.058	0.010
	sig. (2-tailed)	0.159	0.967	0.496	0.909
	N	138	139	139	138
PC36E	Pearson correlation	−0.040	−0.120	0.076	0.102
	sig. (2-tailed)	0.644	0.157	0.374	0.234
	N	139	140	140	139
PC36F	Pearson correlation	0.059	−0.101	0.124	0.071
	sig. (2-tailed)	0.488	0.231	0.142	0.407
	N	140	141	141	140

Note: PC = Personal characteristics CM = Classroom management OI = Organizing for instruction ID = Instructional delivery A = Assessment
[a]The wording of each question can be found in Appendix B.
*$p < .05$ **$p < .01$

The Survey

Perceptions of School Leaders on Qualities of Effective Teachers

This questionnaire is being used as part of a study on qualities of effective teachers and interviewing. Your responses are valuable. This survey should take approximately 30 minutes.

Please return the survey regardless of whether you choose to participate. Check below all applicable items.

_____ I decline to participate in the survey.

_____ I would like a summary of the survey's findings and a draft of the interview protocol.
Please e-mail them to me at _____.

PART I

Directions: Please respond to the following questions.

1. Have you interviewed or participated in an interview to select a teacher in the past year?

   ❑ Yes (please continue)   ❑ No (stop here and return the form)

2. In what state/area do you work?

   ❑ CT, ME, MA, NH, RI, VT
   ❑ DE, MD, NJ, NY, PA, DC
   ❑ AL, AR, FL, GA, KY, LA, MS, NC, SC, TN, VA, WV
   ❑ IA, IL, IN, KS, MI, MN, MO, NE, ND, OH, SD, WI
   ❑ AZ, NM, OK, TX
   ❑ AK, CO, CA, HI, ID, MT, NV, OR, UT, WA, WY

3. What term best describes your professional position?

   ❑ Principal   ❑ Assistant Principal   ❑ Other _____

4. What is the context of your school/worksite?

   ❑ Rural   ❑ Suburban   ❑ Urban

5. Indicate the grade level of the positions you most commonly are holding interviews to fill.

   ❑ PreK–Grade 5   ❑ Grades 6–8   ❑ Grades 9–12

6. How many years have you been an administrator?

   ❑ 1   ❑ 2   ❑ 3   ❑ 4   ❑ 5   ❑ 6   ❑ 7
   ❑ 8   ❑ 9   ❑ 10   ❑ 11   ❑ 12   ❑ 13   ❑ 14
   ❑ 15   ❑ 16   ❑ 17   ❑ 18   ❑ 19   ❑ 20   ❑ 21
   ❑ 22   ❑ 23   ❑ 24   ❑ 25   ❑ 26+ Please state _____

7. Approximately how many teacher interviews did you conduct/participate in from fall 2002 to fall 2003?

- ❏ Fewer than 10
- ❏ 11–20
- ❏ 21–30
- ❏ 31–40
- ❏ 41–50
- ❏ More than 50

8. Approximately what percentage of teacher applicants did you interview in 2002–2003 who were novice teachers (3 years experience or less)?

- ❏ 0–20%
- ❏ 21–40%
- ❏ 41–60%
- ❏ 61–80%
- ❏ 81–100%

9. Does your school district offer training on how to conduct teacher selection interviews?

- ❏ Yes   ❏ No

PART II **Directions:** Please indicate how typical each item is when you conduct/participate in an interview.	**Often**	**Sometimes**	**Rarely**
10. Use multiple interviewers	❏	❏	❏
11 Have prepared questions	❏	❏	❏
12. Use a structured interview	❏	❏	❏
13. Ask the same questions to each applicant interviewing for the same position	❏	❏	❏
14. Use a scoring guide or rubric for the responses	❏	❏	❏
15. Determine the desired qualities an applicant would have in order to fulfill the job responsibilities before interviewing begins	❏	❏	❏
16. Take notes during the interview	❏	❏	❏
17. Ask applicants how they would respond to a hypothetical situation	❏	❏	❏
18. Ask applicants to describe how they have responded to situations in the past	❏	❏	❏
19. Use icebreaker or warm-up questions	❏	❏	❏

20. What is your primary source for interview questions?
- ❏ Other administrators   ❏ School district list   ❏ Books   ❏ Commercial product

21. What was your primary way of learning to interview?
- ❏ Other administrators   ❏ School district inservice training   ❏ College course
- ❏ National/state workshop   ❏ Commercial product-related training

22. What is your gender?
- ❏ Female   ❏ Male

PART III

Directions: This survey is designed to help associate statements describing teacher applicants' responses with administrators' judgment of the strength of the statements. Under each boldfaced question are six statements summarizing the responses different teacher applicants may offer to the same question. Consider what type of teacher applicant is likely to make such a statement. Circle only one selection for each statement.

There are four levels for your consideration:

1 – Unsatisfactory (U). *This applicant does not have what it takes to be an effective teacher.*

2 – Developing (D). *This applicant has the makings for a good teacher but is not there yet.*

3 – Proficient (P). *This applicant is most likely a good, solid teacher.*

4 – Exemplary (E). *This applicant is likely a highly effective teacher.*

	U	D	P	E
23. What do you find most rewarding about teaching?				
a. Does not communicate his or her thoughts clearly	1	2	3	4
b. Communicates with clarity and offers examples	1	2	3	4
c. Communicates an idealistic but ungrounded view of teaching	1	2	3	4
d. Communicates with useful concrete and abstract examples	1	2	3	4
e. Communicates a broad idea that lacks specificity	1	2	3	4
f. Communicates a passion for seeing students enjoying learning	1	2	3	4

24. Tell me what you do with students during the first few weeks of the school year with them to establish a positive classroom environment.				
a. Builds a classroom community through student ownership	1	2	3	4
b. Offers limited opportunities for students to practice routines	1	2	3	4
c. Lacks specific examples of how they build rapport with students	1	2	3	4
d. Introduces rules only once and expects students to follow them	1	2	3	4
e. Spends time at the start of the school year reinforcing routines so students can work independently	1	2	3	4
f. Responds to students who are off task and redirects them	1	2	3	4

25. Share with me your long- and short-term planning process. Think about a lesson you recently taught and describe how you planned for it. At the beginning of the school year, how did you plan to address the required _____ (insert name of state standards) objectives for your grade/subject level?				
a. Treats long- and short-term planning as isolated planning functions	1	2	3	4
b. Does not make long-range plans or is unfamiliar with the concept	1	2	3	4
c. Prioritizes instruction by referring to plans	1	2	3	4
d. Uses both long- and short-term planning, relying heavily on short-term	1	2	3	4
e. Uses planning to help consolidate facts into broader concepts	1	2	3	4
f. Indicates that long-range planning is not useful as there are too many interruptions in the school year	1	2	3	4

1–Unsatisfactory (U)   2–Developing (D)   3–Proficient (P)   4–Exemplary (E)

	U	D	P	E

26. Describe how you engage students in their learning.

	U	D	P	E
a. Modifies activities to address student needs	1	2	3	4
b. Systematically designs differentiated learning activities	1	2	3	4
c. Has a "one size fits all" approach to instruction	1	2	3	4
d. Provides some activities designed to capitalize on student interest	1	2	3	4
e. Provides examples of how he or she achieves high levels of active student engagement	1	2	3	4
f. Does not think school should have to cater to student interests	1	2	3	4

27. Share with me a time you had difficulty with a particular student's behavior and what you did to address it.

	U	D	P	E
a. Works with the student and others (e.g., families, guidance counselors) to help the student meet expectations	1	2	3	4
b. Disciplines students using punitive measures	1	2	3	4
c. Focuses on the need for strict discipline measures	1	2	3	4
d. Reinforces the behavior expectations	1	2	3	4
e. Refers students to the office if he or she does not improve during the class period	1	2	3	4
f. Provides an example where a contributing factor was the teacher's actions	1	2	3	4

28. Explain how you share your grading system with students and families. How do students know how well they are doing? How do you let parents know what grades are based upon?

	U	D	P	E
a. Uses a limited variety of ongoing and culminating assessments	1	2	3	4
b. Grades a variety of assignments and more formal assessments	1	2	3	4
c. Has a mechanism in place for explaining the grading system when new students enter the class during the year (e.g., a welcome pack)	1	2	3	4
d. Provides adequate feedback on performance	1	2	3	4
e. Interprets and communicates student progress through regularly timed reports that are issued in addition to the school's marking period	1	2	3	4
f. Prefers to base grades solely on culminating assignments (e.g., tests)	1	2	3	4

29. Think about a unit you have taught. Tell me why you selected particular teaching strategies to address the curriculum.

	U	D	P	E
a. Diagnostically uses a wide range of instructional strategies to optimize student learning	1	2	3	4
b. Refers to a few instructional strategies he or she knows well	1	2	3	4
c. Selects strategies that appeal to students' learning styles	1	2	3	4
d. Considers the resources available to teach using various strategies	1	2	3	4
e. Works with another teacher who suggested the strategies would work well to teach the unit to students	1	2	3	4
f. Credits the textbook with the selection of strategies	1	2	3	4

	U	D	P	E

30. Tell me how your assessment practices accommodate students' learning needs.

a. Analyzes past student performance on assessments to determine how the student best demonstrates his or her knowledge   1   2   3   4

b. Assesses all students the same   1   2   3   4

c. Gives modified assessments when they are prepared by the special education teacher   1   2   3   4

d. Differentiates as appropriate for students of all ability levels   1   2   3   4

e. Changes some aspects of the assessment based on the instruction students received   1   2   3   4

f. Accommodates only when there is an IEP or 504 plan being enforced   1   2   3   4

31. Give an example of how you establish and maintain rapport with your students.

a. Watches TV shows that are popular with students   1   2   3   4

b. Provides examples of caring about individual students in and out of school   1   2   3   4

c. Says it is hard to relate to students who are so different from the teacher or other students he or she has taught   1   2   3   4

d. Focuses on the teacher role of controlling students   1   2   3   4

e. Offers examples of involvement with students outside of contract hours (e.g., club, coaching, attendance at extracurricular events)   1   2   3   4

f. Interacts and knows students by group interests   1   2   3   4

32. Describe how you promote high expectations for student achievement during your instructional time.

a. Offers examples of what meeting varying levels of expectation looks like on particular assignments   1   2   3   4

b. Is enthusiastic about learning   1   2   3   4

c. Encourages students to participate in their learning   1   2   3   4

d. Places sole responsibility for student success on the student   1   2   3   4

e. Believes that different students have different needs at different times, so high expectations reflect student differences   1   2   3   4

f. Suggests that student achievement is the job of the student and is influenced slightly by the teacher   1   2   3   4

33. How does your use of instructional time demonstrate that learning is students' primary purpose?

a. Focuses on how learning time may be interrupted by external events, so the teacher verbally reminds students to pay attention   1   2   3   4

b. Talks about cutting short lessons because noninstructional activities use up the time   1   2   3   4

c. Considers the time it takes the educator to teach and the student to learn when allocating time   1   2   3   4

d. Offers examples of how a high percentage of the day is devoted to instruction, such as taking advantage of teachable moments   1   2   3   4

e. Gives a basic answer about how much time is spent in class   1   2   3   4

f. Is flexible in time use to ensure students learn   1   2   3   4

1–Unsatisfactory (U)   2–Developing (D)   3–Proficient (P)   4–Exemplary (E)

	U	D	P	E

34. How do you use technology during your instruction?

a. Offers examples of how technology and other related resources are integrated
into meaningful lessons — 1   2   3   4

b. Is uncomfortable with technology — 1   2   3   4

c. Creates tasks to increase students' proficiency and expertise in appropriately
using the technology — 1   2   3   4

d. Uses available technology as appropriate to instructional objectives — 1   2   3   4

e. Applies technology inappropriately in the example — 1   2   3   4

f. Fails to provide an example of authentic student work using technology — 1   2   3   4

35. Pick a topic in your subject area that is often difficult for students to understand. Tell me what the topic is and how you explain it to students, and share with me directions for an activity you do to help further students' understanding of that topic.

a. Provides an inadequate answer that demonstrates some knowledge — 1   2   3   4

b. Offers plenty of instructional examples and guided practice — 1   2   3   4

c. Gives confusing examples and directions in the example selected — 1   2   3   4

d. Communicates the topic with a lack of clarity — 1   2   3   4

e. Provides an example in which the class was addressed as a group on the topic and
then the teacher targeted specific individuals for additional explanation as necessary — 1   2   3   4

f. Uses clear examples and step-by-step directions — 1   2   3   4

36. Think about a lesson that did not meet your expectations, despite planning and preparation. Tell me what you considered when planning to readdress the topic with your students and describe how you altered your approach.

a. Focuses on non-teacher-related issues — 1   2   3   4

b. Addresses the issue with limited evidence of reflection — 1   2   3   4

c. Reflects to improve teaching — 1   2   3   4

d. Reflects on the teaching and the students to improve learning — 1   2   3   4

e. Focuses on what the students did wrong — 1   2   3   4

f. Describes reteaching the concept another way so students could learn — 1   2   3   4

Please return the survey in the self-addressed stamped envelope provided.

Thank you for your participation!

References

Age Discrimination in Employment Act of 1967 (ADEA), Pub. L. 90-202 (codified in 29 U.S.C. §621).

Americans with Disabilities Act of 1990 (ADA), Pub. L. 101-336.

Anstey, E., & Mercer, E. O. (1956). *Interviewing for the selection of staff.* London: George Allen & Unwin, Ltd.

Bauer, T. N., Truxillo, D. M., Sanchez, R. J., Craig, J. M., Ferrara, P., & Campion, M. A. (2001). Applicant reactions to selection: Development of Selection Procedural Justice Scale (SPJS). *Personnel Psychology, 54,* 387–419.

Berliner, D. C. (1986). In pursuit of the expert pedagogue. *Educational Researcher, 15*(7), 5–13.

Black, R. S., & Howard-Jones, A. (2000). Reflections on best and worst teachers: An experiential perspective of teaching. *Journal of Research and Development in Education, 34*(1), 1–12.

Bloom, B. S. (1984, May). The search for methods of group instruction as effective as one-to-one tutoring. *Educational Leadership, 41*(8), 4–17.

Brtek, M. D., & Motowidlo, S. J. (2002). Effects of procedure and outcome accountability on interview validity. *Journal of Applied Psychology, 87*(1), 185–191.

Buckley, M. R., & Eder, R. W. (1989, May). The first impression. *Personnel Administrator, 34*(5), 71–74.

Burnett, J. R., Fan, C., Motowidlo, S. J., & DeGroot, T. (1998). Interview notes and validity. *Personnel Psychology, 51*(2), 375–396.

Buttram, J. L., & Waters, J. T. (1997). Improving America's schools through standards-based education. *NASSP Bulletin, 81*(590), 1–5.

Camphire, G. (2001). Are our teachers good enough? *SEDLetter, 13*(2). Available from http://www.sedl.org/pubs/sedletter/v13n02/v13n02.pdf

Campion, M. A., Palmer, D. K., & Campion, J. E. (1997). A review of structure in the selection interview. *Personnel Psychology, 50,* 655–702.

Cascio, W. F. (1998). *Managing human resources: Productivity, quality of work life, profits* (5th ed.). Boston: Irwin McGraw-Hill.

Cascio, W. F. (2003). *Managing human resources: Productivity, quality of work, life, profits* (6th ed.). Boston: McGraw-Hill/Irwin.

Castetter, W. B. (1996). *The human resource function in educational administration* (6th ed.). Englewood Cliffs, NJ: Merrill.

Cawelti, G. (Ed.) (1999). *Handbook of research on improving student achievement* (2nd ed.). Arlington, VA: Educational Research Service.

Check, J. F. (1999). The perceptions of their former teachers by older adults. *Education, 120*(1), 168–172.

Civil Rights Act of 1964, Title VII, Pub. L. 88-352 (codified in 42 U.S.C. § 2000e).

Collins, J. (2001). *Good to great: Why some companies make the leap—and others don't.* New York: HarperBusiness.

Collinson, V., Killeavy, M., & Stephenson, H. J. (1999). Exemplary teachers: Practicing an ethic of care in England, Ireland, and the United States. *Journal for a Just and Caring Education, 5*(4), 349–366.

Conway, J. M., & Peneno, G. M. (1999). Comparing structured interview question types: Construct validity and applicant reactions. *Journal of Business and Psychology, 13*(4), 485–506.

Corcoran, C. A., & Leahy, R. (2003). Growing professionally through reflective practice. *Kappa Delta Pi Record, 40*(1), 30–33.

Cotton, K. (2000). *Research you can use to improve results.* Portland, OR: Northwest Regional Educational Laboratory; and Alexandria, VA: Association for Supervision and Curriculum Development.

Covino, E. A., & Iwanicki, E. F. (1996). Experienced teachers: Their constructs of effective teaching. *Journal of Personnel Evaluation in Education, 10*(4), 325–363.

Cross, C. T., & Regden, D. W. (2002). Improving teacher quality. *American School Board Journal, 189*(4). Available: http://www.asbj.com/2002/04/0402coverstory2.html

Cruickshank, D. R., & Haefele, D. (2001, February). Good teachers, plural. *Educational Leadership, 58*(5), 26–30.

Cunningham, P. M., & Allington, R. L. (1999). *Classrooms that work: They can all read and write.* New York: Longman.

Darling-Hammond, L. (2000a). *Solving the dilemmas of teacher supply, demand, and standards: How we can ensure a competent, caring, and qualified teacher for every child.* New York: National Commission on Teaching & America's Future.

Darling-Hammond, L. (2000b). Teacher quality and student achievement: A review of state policy evidence. *Educational Policy Analysis Archives, 8*(1). Available: http://epaa.asu.edu/epaa/v8n1/

Darling-Hammond, L. (2001, February). The challenge of staffing our schools. *Educational Leadership, 58*(8), 12–17.

Darling-Hammond, L., Berry, B., & Thoreson, A. (2001). Does teacher certification matter? Evaluating the evidence. *Educational Evaluation and Policy Analysis, 23*(1), 57–77.

De Corte, W. (1999). Weighing job performance predictors to both maximize the quality of the selected workforce and control the level of adverse impact. *Journal of Applied Psychology, 84*(5), 695–702.

Delaney, E. C. (1954). Teacher selection and evaluation: With special attention to the validity of the personal interview and the National Teacher Examinations as used in one selected community (Elizabeth, New Jersey). Doctoral dissertation, Columbia University. Dissertation Abstracts Online (AAG0008645).

Dessler, G. (1997). *Human resource management* (7th ed.). Upper Saddle River, NJ: Prentice Hall.

Dickson, L. A., & Irving, M. M. (2002). An Internet survey: Assessing the extent middle/high school teachers use the Internet to enhance science teaching. *Journal of Computers in Mathematics and Science Teaching, 21*(1), 77–97.

Dill, I., & Dill, V. (1993, March). Describe your favorite teacher. . . . *Educational Leadership, 50*(6), 54–56.

Dipboye, R. L. (1997). Structured selection interviews: Why do they work? Why are they underutilized? In N. Anderson & P. Herriot (Eds.), *International handbook of selection and assessment* (pp. 455–475). New York: J. Wiley.

Dipboye, R. L., & Gaugler, B. B. (1993). Cognitive and behavioral processes in the selection interview. In N. Schmitt & W. C. Borman (Eds.), *Personnel selection in organizations* (pp. 135–170). San Francisco: Jossey-Bass.

Donaldson, G. A. (1990). *Teacher selection and induction.* Reston, VA: National Association of Secondary School Principals.

Dozier, T., & Bertotti, C. (2000). *Eliminating barriers to quality teaching.* Retrieved August 22, 2000, from http://www.ed.gov/teacherquality/awareness.html

Edenborough, R. (1999). *Effective interviewing: A handbook of skills, techniques and applications.* Dover, NH: Kogan Page.

Eder, R. W., & Harris, M. M. (Eds.). (1999). *The employment interview handbook.* Thousand Oaks, CA: Sage Publications.

Edmonton Public Schools. (1993, May). *Qualities of successful teachers.* Draft Document. Edmonton, Aberta, Canada.

Education USA Special Report. (n.d.). *Good teachers: What to look for.* A publication of The National School Public Relations Association.

Educational Review Office. (1998). *The capable teacher.* Available: http://www.ero.govt.nz/Publications/eers1998/98no2hl.htm

Edwards, V. B. (Ed.). (2000). *Quality counts 2000: Who should teach?* Bethesda, MD: Education Week.

Eisner, E. W. (1999). The uses and limits of performance assessment. *Phi Delta Kappan, 80*(9), 658–660.

Ellis, A., West, B. J. , Ryan, A. M., & DeShon, R. (2002). Investigating the use of impression management tactics in structured interviews. *Journal of Applied Psychology, 87,* 1200-1208.

Emley, K., & Ebmeier, H. (1997). The effect of employment interview format on principals' evaluations of teachers. *Journal of Personnel Evaluation in Education, 11*(1), 39–56.

Emmer, E. T., Evertson, C. M., & Anderson, L. M. (1980). Effective classroom management at the beginning of the school year. *The Elementary School Journal, 80*(5), 219–231.

Entwisle, D. R., & Webster, M., Jr. (1973). Research notes: Status factors in expectation raising. [Electronic version]. *Sociology of Education, 46,* 115–125.

Equal Employment Opportunity Act of 1972, Pub. L. 92-261.

Equal Pay Act of 1963 (EPA), Pub. L. 88-38 (codified in 29 U.S.C. § 206(d)).

Family and Medical Leave Act of 1993 (FMLA), Pub. L. 103-3 (codified in 29 U.S.C. § 2612).

Ferguson, P., & Womack, S. T. (1993). The impact of subject matter and education coursework on teaching performance. *Journal of Teacher Education, 44,* 55–63.

Fetler, M. (1999). High school staff characteristics and mathematics test results. *Educational Policy Analysis Archives, 7*(9). Available: http://epaa.asu.edu/epaa/v7n9.html

Freel, A. (1998). Achievement in urban schools: What makes the difference? *The Education Digest, 64*(1), 17–22.

Gay, L. R. (1987). *Educational research: Competencies for Analysis and Application* (3rd ed.). New York: MacMillan.

Gerald, D. E., & Hussar, W. J. (2003). *Projections of education statistics to 2013* (NCES Publication No. NCES 2004-013). Washington, DC: U.S. Department of Education, Office of Educational Research and Improvement.

Glass, C. S. (2001). Factors influencing teaching strategies used with children who display attention deficit hyperactivity disorder characteristics. *Education, 122*(1), 70–80.

Glass, G. V. (2002). Teacher characteristics. In A. Molnar (Ed.), *School reform proposals: The research evidence* (pp. 155–174). Greenwich, CT: Information Age Pub.

Goldhaber, D. D., & Brewer, D. J. (2000). Does teacher certification matter? High school teacher certification status and student achievement. *Educational Evaluation and Policy Analysis, 22*(2), 129–145.

Good, T. L., & Brophy, J. E. (1997). *Looking in classrooms* (7th ed.). New York: Longman.

Goodrich, H. (1996). Understanding rubrics. *Educational Leadership, 54*(4), 4–17.

Gronlund, N. E. (2003). *Assessment of student achievement* (7th ed.). Boston: Allyn & Bacon.

Grossman, P., Valencia, S., Evans, K., Thompson, C., Martin, S., & Place, N. (2000). *Transitions into teaching: Learning to teach writing in teacher education and beyond.* Available: http://cela.albany.edu/reports/transitions/main.html

Guskey, T. R. (1996). Reporting on student learning: Lessons from the past—Prescriptions for the future. In T. R. Guskey (Ed.), *Communicating student learning: ASCD yearbook 1996.* Alexandria, VA: Association for Supervision and Curriculum Development.

Haberman, M. (1995a). Selecting "star" teachers for children and youth in urban poverty. *Phi Delta Kappan, 76*(10), 777–782.

Haberman, M. (1995b). *Star teachers of children in poverty.* West Lafayette, IN: Kappa Delta Pi.

Haertel, E. H. (1999). Performance assessment and education reform. *Phi Delta Kappan, 80*(9), 662–666.

Hanushek, E. (1971). Teacher characteristics and gains in student achievement: Estimation using micro data. *American Economic Review, 61*(2), 280–288.

Hawk, P. P., Coble, C. R., & Swanson, M. (1985). Certification: Does it matter? *Journal of Teacher Education, 36*(3), 13–15.

Henke, R. R., Chen, X., & Geis, S. (2000). *Progress through the teacher pipeline: 1992–93 college graduates and elementary/secondary school teaching as of 1997* (NCES Publication No. 2000-152). Washington, DC: U.S. Dept. of Education, Office of Educational Research and Improvement.

Hindman, J. L. (2004). The connection between qualities of effective teachers and selection interviews: The development of a teacher selection interview protocol. The College of William and Mary, Williamsburg, Virginia. *Dissertation Abstracts International* (UMI No. 3118184).

Hirsch, E. D., Jr. (2000). The tests we need. *Education Week, 19*(21), 40–41, 64.

Holahan, P. J., Jurkat, M. P., & Friedman, E. A. (2000). Evaluation of a mentor teacher model for enhancing mathematics instruction through the use of computers [abstract]. *Journal of Research on Technology Education, 32*(3). Available: http://www.iste.org/inhouse/publications/jrte/32/3/abstracts/holahan.cfm?Section=JRTE_32_3

Hoy, A. W., & Hoy, W. K. (2003). *Instructional leadership: A learning-centered guide.* Boston: Allyn & Bacon.

Huffcutt, A. I., Conway, J. M., Roth, P. L., & Stone, N. J. (2001). Identification and meta-analytic assessment of psychological constructs measured in employment interviews. *Journal of Applied Psychology, 86*(5), 897–913.

Huffcutt, A. I., Weekley, J. A., Wiesner, W. H., DeGroot, T. G., & Jones, C. (2001). A comparison of situational and behavior description interview questions for higher-level positions. *Personnel Psychology, 54*(3), 619–644.

Hussar, W. J. (1999). *Predicting the need for newly hired teachers in the United States to 2008–09* (NCES Publication No. NCES 1999-026). Washington, DC: U.S. Government Printing Office.

Hussar, W. J., & Gerald, D. E. (2004). *Pocket Projections of Education Statistics to 2013* (NCES Publication No. NCES 2004-019). Washington, DC: U.S. Department of Education, National Center for Education Statistics.

Ingersoll, R. M. (2001). *Teacher turnover, teacher shortages, and the organization of schools* (Document R-01-1). Seattle: University of Washington, Center for the Study of Teaching and Policy.

International Society for Technology in Education. (n.d.). *Overview: Research on IT [informational technology] in education.* Available: http://www.iste.org/Content/NavigationMenu/Research/Reports/Research_on_Technology_in_Education_2000_/Overview/Overview_Research_on_IT_in_Education.htm

Johnson, B. L. (1997). An organizational analysis of multiple perspectives of effective teaching: Implications for teacher evaluation. *Journal of Personnel Evaluation in Education, 11*(1), 69–87.

Kiker, D. S., & Motowidlo, S. J. (1998). Effects of rating strategy on interdimensional variance, reliability, and validity of interview ratings. *Journal of Applied Psychology, 83*(5), 763–768.

Kirkpatrick, L. A., & Feeney, B. C. (2001). *A simple guide to SPSS for Windows: For version 8.0, 9.0, and 10.0.* Belmont, CA: Wadsworth Thompson Learning.

Kohn, A. (1996). What to look for in a classroom. *Educational Leadership, 54*(1), 54–55.

Laczko-Kerr, I., & Berliner, D. C. (2002). The effectiveness of "Teach for America" and other under-certified teachers on student academic achievement: A case of harmful public policy, *Education Policy Analysis Archives, 10*(37). Available: http://epaa.asu.edu/epaa/v10n37/

Langer, J. (2001). Beating the odds: Teaching middle and high school students to read and write well. *American Educational Research Journal, 38*(4), 837–880.

Lederman, N. G., & Niess, M. L. (2001). An attempt to anchor our moving targets. *School Science and Mathematics, 101*(2), 57–60.

Litwin, M. S. (1995). *How to measure survey reliability and validity.* Thousand Oaks, CA: Sage Publications.

Livingston, A., & Wirt, J. (2004). *The condition of education 2004 in brief* (NCES Publication No. 2004-076). U.S. Department of Education, National Center for Education Statistics. Washington, DC: U.S. Government Printing Office.

Macan, T. H., & Dipboye, R. L. (1994). The effects of the application on processing information from the employment interview. *Journal of Applied Social Psychology, 24*(14), 1291–1314.

Marzano, R. J., Norford, J. S., Paynter, D. E., Pickering, D. J., & Gaddy, B. B. (2001). *A handbook for classroom instruction that works.* Alexandria, VA: Association for Supervision and Curriculum Development.

Marzano, R. J., Pickering, D., & McTighe, J. (1993). *Assessing student outcomes: Performance assessment using the dimensions of learning model.* Alexandria, VA: Association for Supervision and Curriculum Development.

Mason, D. A., Schroeter, D. D., Combs, R. K., & Washington, K. (1992). Assigning average-achieving eighth graders to advanced mathematics classes in an urban junior high. *The Elementary School Journal, 92*(5), 587–599.

Maurer, S. D., & Fay, C. (1988). Effect of situational interviews, conventional structured interviews, and training on interview rating agreement: An experimental analysis. *Personnel Psychology, 41,* 329–344.

Maurer, S. D., & Lee, T. W., (2000). Accuracy of the situational interview in rating multiple job candidates. *Journal of Business and Psychology, 15*(1), 73–96.

McBer, H. (2000). *Research into teacher effectiveness: A model of teacher effectiveness.* (Research Report #216). Nottingham, England: Department for Education and Employment.

McDaniel, M. A., Whetzel, D. L., Schmidt, F. L., & Maurer, S. D. (1994). The validity of employment interviews: a comprehensive review and meta-analysis. *Journal of Applied Psychology, 79*(4), 599–616.

McEwan, E. K. (2001). *10 traits of highly effective teachers: How to hire, coach, and mentor successful teachers.* Thousand Oaks, CA: Corwin Press.

McFarland, L. A., Ryan, A. M., & Kriska, S. D. (2002). Field study investigation of applicant use of influence tactics in a selection interview. *The Journal of Psychology, 136*(4), 383–398.

Mendro, R. L., Jordon, H. R., Gomez, E., Anderson, M. C., & Bembry, K. L. (1998, April). *Longitudinal teacher effects on student achievement and their relation to school and project evaluation.* Paper presented at the Annual Meeting of the Educational Research Association, San Diego, CA.

Middendorf, C. H., & Macan, T. H. (2002). Note-taking in the employment interview: Effects on recall and judgments. *Journal of Applied Psychology, 87*(2), 293–303.

National Association of Secondary School Principals. (1997). Students say: What makes a good teacher? *NASSP Bulletin, 6*(5), 15–17.

No Child Left Behind Act of 2001, Pub. L. No. 107-110, 115 Stat. 1425 (codified in 20 U.S.C. §6301).

Northwest Regional Education Laboratory. (2001). *Understanding motivation and supporting teacher renewal.* Available: http://www.nwrel.org/qualityteaching/products/UnderstandingMotivation.pdf

Panasuk, R., Stone, W., & Todd, J. (2002). Lesson planning strategy for effective mathematics teaching. *Education, 22*(2), 714, 808–827.

Pawlas, G. E. (1995). The structured interview: Three dozen questions to ask prospective teachers. *NASSP Bulletin, 79*(567), 62–65.

Peart, N. A., & Campbell, F. A. (1999). At-risk students' perceptions of teacher effectiveness. *Journal for a Just and Caring Education, 5*(3), 269–284.

Perkins, M. Y. (1998). An analysis of teacher interview questions and practices used by middle school principals. Doctoral dissertation, Virginia Polytechnic Institute and State University. *Digital Library Archives* (URN: etd-32398-16236).

Peterson, K. D. (2002). *Effective teacher hiring: A guide to getting the best.* Alexandria, VA: Association for Supervision and Curriculum Development.

Pulakos, E. D., & Schmitt, N. (1995). Experience-based and situational interview questions: Studies of validity. *Personnel Psychology, 48*(2), 289–308.

Pulakos, E. D., Schmitt, N., Whitney, D. J., & Smith, M. (1996). Individual differences in interviewer ratings: The impact of standardization, consensus discussion, and sampling error on the validity of a structured interview. *Personnel Psychology, 49*(1), 85–102.

Ralph, E. G., Kesten, C., Lang, H., & Smith, D. (1998). Hiring new teachers: What do school districts look for? [Electronic version]. *Journal of Teacher Education, 49*(1), 47–57.

Rehabilitation Act of 1973, Pub. L. 93-112 (codified in 29 U.S.C. § 791 et seq.).

Reynolds, A. (1992). What is competent beginning teaching? A review of the literature. *Review of Educational Research, 62*(1), 1–35.

Rockman et al. (1998). Powerful tools for schooling: Second year study of the laptop program [executive summary]. Report for the Microsoft Corporation. Available: http://rockman.com/projects/laptop/laptop2exec.htm

Ross, J. A., Cousins, J. B., Gadalla, T., & Hannay, L. (1999). Administrative assignment of teachers in restructuring secondary schools: The effect of out-of-field course responsibility on teacher efficacy. *Educational Administration Quarterly, 35*(5), 782–805.

Rowan, B., Chiang, F. S., & Miller, R. J. (1997). Using research on employees' performance to study the effects of teachers on students' achievement. *Sociology of Education, 70,* 256–284.

Ruiz, C. M., & Sperow, J. L. (1997, Summer). *School law quarterly: The hiring process.* San Francisco: Authors.

Sanders, W. L., & Horn, S. P. (1998). Research findings from the Tennessee Value-Added Assessment System (TVAAS) database: Implications for educational evaluation and research. *Journal of Personnel Evaluation in Education, 12*(3), 247–256.

Sanders, W. L., & Rivers, J. C. (1996). *Cumulative and residual effects of teachers on future student academic achievement* (Research Progress Report). Knoxville, TN: University of Tennessee Value-Added Research and Assessment Center.

Scherer, M. (2001, May). Improving the quality of the teaching force: A conversation with David C. Berliner. *Educational Leadership, 58*(8), 6–10.

Schmidt, F. L., & Rader, M. (1999). Exploring the boundary conditions for interview validity: Meta-analytic validity findings for a new interview type. *Personnel Psychology, 52*(2), 445–464.

Shechtman, Z., & Sansbury, D. (1989). Validation of a group assessment procedure for the selection of teacher-education candidates. *Educational and Psychological Measurement, 49*(3), 653–661.

Shellard, E., & Protheroe, N. (2000). *The informed educator: Effective teaching: How do we know it when we see it?* Arlington, VA: Educational Research Services.

Sizer, T. R. (1999, September). No two are quite alike. *Educational Leadership, 57*(1), 6–11.

Springbett, B. M. (1958). Factors affecting the final decision in the employment interview. *Canadian Journal of Psychology, 12*(1), 13–22.

Stevens, C. K. (1998). Antecedents of interview interactions, interviewers' ratings, and applicants' reactions. *Personnel Psychology, 51*(1), 55–85.

Stronge, J. H. (2002). *Qualities of effective teachers.* Alexandria, VA: Association for Supervision and Curriculum Development.

Stronge, J. H., Tucker, P. D., & Hindman, J. L. (2004). *Handbook for qualities of effective teachers.* Alexandria, VA: Association for Supervision and Curriculum Development.

Stronge, J. H., Tucker, P. D., & Ward, T. J. (2003, April). *Teacher effectiveness and student learning: What do good teachers do?* Presentation at the American Educational Research Association, Chicago.

Stronge, J. H., & Ward, T. J. (2002). *Alexandria City Public Schools teacher effectiveness study.* Report presented to the Alexandria City School Board, Alexandria, VA.

Taylor, P. J., & Small, B. (2002). Asking applicants what they would do versus what they did do: A meta-analytic comparison of situational and past behaviour employment interview questions. *Journal of Occupational and Organizational Psychology, 75*(3), 277–294.

Thomas, J. A., & Montgomery, P. (1998). On becoming a good teacher: Reflective practice with regard to children's voices. *Journal of Teacher Education, 49*(5), 372–380.

Tomlinson, C. A. (1999). *The differentiated classroom: Responding to the needs of all learners.* Alexandria, VA: Association for Supervision and Curriculum Development.

Tucker, P. D., & Stronge, J. H. (2005). *Linking teacher evaluation and student learning.* Alexandria, VA: Association for Supervision and Curriculum Development.

U.S. Department of Education. (1998). *Promising practices: New ways to improve teacher quality.* Available: http://www.ed.gov/pubs/PromPractice/promprac.pdf

U.S. Department of Education. (2001). *The condition of education 2001* (NCES Publication No. 2001-072). Washington, DC: U.S. Government Printing Office.

U.S. Department of Education. (2002, June 6). *Improving teacher quality state grants: Title II, Part A, non-regulatory draft guidance.* Available: http://www.pen.k12.va.us/VDOE/nclb/guidance/PreliminaryGuidanceRelatingtoImprovingTeacherQuality.pdf.

Virginia Department of Education. (2002). *Implementing the No Child Left Behind Act of 2001: Questions and answers.* Richmond, VA: Author.

Walberg, H. J. (1984, May). Improving the productivity of America's schools. *Educational Leadership, 41*(8), 19–27.

Walker, M. H. (1998). 3 basics for better student output. *The Education Digest, 63*(9), 15–18.

Wang, M. C., Haertel, G. D., & Walberg, H. J. (1994). What helps students learn? *Educational Leadership, 51*(4), 74–79.

Weisberg, H. F., Krosnick, J. A., & Bowen, B. D. (1996). *An introduction to survey research, polling, and data analysis* (3rd ed.). Thousand Oaks, CA: Sage Publications.

Wenglinsky, H. (2000). *How teaching matters: Bringing the classroom back into discussions of teacher quality.* Princeton, NJ: Millikan Family Foundation and Educational Testing Service.

Williamson, L. G., Campion, J. E., Malos, S. B., Roehling, M. V., & Campion, M. A. (1997). Employment interview on trial: Linking interview structure with litigation outcomes. *Journal of Applied Psychology, 82*(6), 900–912.

Wubbels, T., Levy, J., & Brekelmans, M. (1997, April). Paying attention to relationships. *Educational Leadership, 54*(7), 82–86.

Yin, C. C., & Kwok, T. T. (1999). Multimodels of teacher effectiveness: Implications for research. *The Journal of Educational Research, 92*(3), 141–158.

Young, I. P., Rinehart, J. S., & Baits, D. M. (1997). Age discrimination: Impact of chronological age and perceived position demands on teacher screening decisions. *Journal of Research and Development in Education, 30*(2), 103–112.

Index

Page references for figures are indicated by an *f*.

About the Authors

James H. Stronge is Heritage Professor in the Educational Policy, Planning, and Leadership Area at the College of William and Mary in Williamsburg, Virginia. Among his primary research interests are teacher effectiveness and student success, and teacher and administrator performance evaluation. He has worked with numerous school districts and state and national educational organizations to design and develop evaluation systems for teachers, administrators, superintendents, and support personnel. He is the author or coauthor of numerous articles, books, and technical reports on teacher quality and performance evaluation, including *Linking Teacher Evaluation and Student Learning* (2005), *Qualities of Effective Teachers* (2002), and *Handbook for Qualities of Effective Teachers* (2004). Stronge received his PhD in educational administration and planning from the University of Alabama. He has been a teacher, counselor, and district-level administrator. He can be contacted at the College of William and Mary, School of Education, PO Box 8795, Williamsburg, VA 23187-8795; phone: (757) 221-2339; e-mail: jhstro@wm.edu; Web site: http://jhstro.people.wm.edu.

Jennifer L. Hindman is an educational consultant with Teacher Quality Resources, LLC. She consults in the areas of teacher selection; teacher effectiveness; and teacher, educational specialist, and administrator performance evaluation. She coauthored *Handbook for Qualities of Effective Teachers* (2004) with James H. Stronge and Pamela D. Tucker. Her work has been published by *Educational Leadership, Principal Leadership,* and the National Center for Homeless Education. Her research interests include teacher effectiveness and teacher selection. She has conducted numerous workshops on the enhancement of teacher effectiveness in science, parental involvement, and resources for practitioners supporting students experiencing homelessness. Hindman received her PhD in educational policy, planning, and leadership at the College of William and Mary. She has been a middle school teacher and a science specialist. She may be contacted via e-mail at jhindman@teacherqualityresources.com; phone: (757) 564-1294.

A Guide to the CD-ROM

The CD-ROM accompanying this book provides downloadable versions of the Teacher Quality Index interview protocols. The forms are compatible with both PC and Macintosh computers and are presented in the Portable Document Format (PDF). *Please note:* **Once you open the seal on the CD-ROM, this book and the CD-ROM are nonrefundable.**

Disk Contents

Form 1 TQI Screening Interview—Standard Format

Form 2 TQI Screening Interview—Interviewer's Choice Format

Form 3 TQI Building-Level Interview—Standard Format

Form 4 TQI Building-Level Interview—Novice Format
For applicants with full-time teaching experience of one year or less

Form 5 TQI Building-Level Interview—Interviewer's Choice Format

Adobe® Acrobat Reader® version 7.0.5 for Windows and Macintosh is included for your convenience. The most current version(s) of the Adobe Reader software are available for download at www.adobe.com.

Minimum System Requirements

Windows:
- Intel® Pentium processor
- Microsoft® Windows 98 Second Edition, Windows Millennium Edition, Windows NT® 4.0 with Service Pack 6, Windows 2000 with Service Pack 2, Windows XP Professional or Home Edition, Windows XP Tablet PC Edition
- 32MB of RAM (64MB recommended)
- 60MB of available hard-disk space
- Internet Explorer 5.01, 5.5, 6.0, or 6.1

Macintosh:
- PowerPC® G3 processor
- Mac OS X v.10.2.2–10.3
- 32MB of RAM with virtual memory on (64MB recommended)
- 30MB of available hard disk space
- HFS formatted hard drive

Terms of Use

The forms on the CD-ROM are protected by copyright and all rights are reserved by the Association for Supervision and Curriculum Development. Up to 100 copies of the forms may be used for educational, nonprofit use only. Validity depends on strictly limited use of the forms.

Related ASCD Resources: Effective Teachers

At the time of publication, the following ASCD resources were available; for the most up-to-date information about ASCD resources, go to www.ascd.org. ASCD stock numbers are noted in parentheses.

Audio

Interviewing Protocols for Identifying High-Quality Teachers by James H. Stronge (audiotape: #205081; CD: #505105)

CD-ROM

Analyzing Teaching (two-disc set with four lessons) (#503367)

Networks

Visit the ASCD Web site (www.ascd.org) and click on About ASCD and then on Networks for information about professional educators who have formed groups around topics, including "Quality Education," "Mentoring Leadership and Resources," and "Performance Assessment for Leadership." Look in the "Network Directory" for current facilitators' addresses and phone numbers.

Print Products

ASCD Infobrief 22 (August 2000): *Ensuring Teacher Quality* by Carol Tell (#100297)

Effective Teacher Hiring: A Guide to Getting the Best by Kenneth D. Peterson (#102047)

Handbook for Qualities of Effective Teachers by James H. Stronge, Pamela D. Tucker, and Jennifer L. Hindman (#104135)

Qualities of Effective Teachers by James H. Stronge (#102007)

Teacher Evaluation/Teacher Portfolios ASCD Topic Pack (#197202)

Video Programs

The Teacher Series, Tapes 1–3 (three videotapes, plus a facilitator's guide) (#401088)

Qualities of Effective Teachers (three video programs on one DVD, plus a facilitator's guide) (#604423)

For additional resources, visit us on the World Wide Web (http://www.ascd.org), send an e-mail message to member@ascd.org, call the ASCD Service Center (1-800-933-ASCD or 703-578-9600, then press 2), send a fax to 703-575-5400, or write to Information Services, ASCD, 1703 N. Beauregard St., Alexandria, VA 22311-1714 USA.